Tudor History under Pressure

Elnora Abshire

Abstract

When Henry Tudor defeated king Richard III at Bosworth Field in 1485, he claimed the English throne as Henry VII by right of conquest and dynastic descent. Although the crown worked assiduously to diffuse this perception and ensure that the Tudors' claim appeared legitimate, many of Henry VII's subjects perceived him as a usurper and a tyrant throughout his reign. Details of Henry VII's regime were recorded in several contemporary narrative accounts, most notably during the reign of his son Henry VIII. Since Henry VIII's claim to the throne was through his father, he had to straddle a fine line between distancing his reign from the previous regime and stressing dynastic continuity. This created a conundrum for contemporary writers and scholars looking back at the beginning of the Tudor dynasty during the tumultuous political climate of Henry VIII's reign in the 1510s and 1530s. Through an analysis of Polydore Vergil's *Anglica Historia* as well as Thomas More's *History of King Richard III* and *Utopia,* this thesis explores the links between the political climate of Henry VIII's court and the choices that contemporary writers made in writing and publishing their representations of the early Tudors. Ultimately, it was fear and pressure that ensured that Polydore Vergil and Sir Thomas More altered their narratives and censored any open accusations of tyranny towards Henry VII and Henry VIII. In both cases, patronage played a large role in shaping the creation of these representations so that the work reflected the wishes of the patron.

Table of Contents

List of Figures

Introduction

When Henry VIII inherited the throne of England at eighteen years of age, a great many of his subjects wholeheartedly believed that this new regime would right the wrongs of the previous century and put an end to tyranny. Thomas More, who was to be Lord Chancellor later on in his career, was one of many who harboured hopes that tyranny would at last see defeat and the new king would ensure that justice prevailed in the face of corruption. In his 1509 coronation ode to Henry VIII, More proclaimed the accession as the "end of [England's] slavery, the beginning of [England's] freedom, the end of sadness, the source of joy."[1] More was not alone in his conviction that Henry VIII would cure the ills of the last few decades. Many believed that the new king represented the end of a multi-decade civil war and the union of the houses of Lancaster and York. His accession also promised a break from the despotism and corruption of Henry VII's reign.

Although the new king succeeded the throne unchallenged and with great expectations, the young Henry still harboured dynastic insecurities that would haunt him throughout his reign. These dynastic insecurities stemmed in large part from the reputation his father, Henry VII, had earned as a usurper and, in the latter years of his reign, as a tyrant. Henry did not want disaffected subjects to rally under the banner of a rival claimant the way they had against his father. Thus, he not only had to prove that his reign marked a departure from the previous one, he also needed to cement his authority and cultivate the loyalty of those alienated by the old regime. These efforts involved the extensive use of propaganda, which, as will be discussed in this thesis, included the adaptation of English historical narratives.

The Tudors were adept at projecting their power and authority through images, various displays of pomp and pageantry, and through the theatrics of mercy and the issuing of royal pardons.[2] The representation of the past was another way the Tudors managed the diffusion of the royal image, an endeavor in which scholars believe they were successful.[3] It is the Tudors'

---

[1] Thomas More, "Epigram 19," *The Complete Works of St. Thomas More, vol. 3.2,* ed. C. H. Miller, L. Bradner, C. A.Lynch, and R. P. Oliver (Yale: Yale University Press, 1984), 101.

[2] K.J. Kesselring, *Mercy and Authority in Tudor England* (Cambridge: Cambridge University Press, 2003).

[3] Alistair Fox, *Politics and Literature in the Reigns of Henry VII and Henry VIII,* (Oxford; New York: Blackwell, 1989), 17; Kevin Sharpe, "Founding a Dynasty, Forging an Image," in *Selling the Tudor Monarchy: Authority and Image in Sixteenth-Century England,* (New Haven; London: Yale University Press, 2009), 61-78.

version of events in the fifteenth and sixteenth centuries that largely prevail to this day, continuing to propagate various elements of the "Tudor myth."[4] This is especially true of the portrayals of King Richard III as a villain, crafted by the likes of Polydore Vergil, Sir Thomas More, and Edward Hall – accounts that all served as inspiration for William Shakespeare's play about the last Plantagenet king. The same can be said for the portrayals of Henry VIII and his father, Henry VII. While some contemporaries may have believed Henry VII to be a tyrant and a usurper of the English crown, the careful crafting of historical representations has masked these impressions, rendering contemporary accounts of his reign rather uneventful in comparison to those of other English monarchs. However, this paper will argue that the writing of these representations and the editorial decisions of their respective authors were influenced by the political climate of Henry VIII's court and the king's dynastic ambitions.

The crown's concerns over legitimacy created a conundrum for contemporary writers and scholars looking back at the beginning of the Tudor dynasty during Henry VIII's reign. They could not openly accuse the father of the current monarch of tyranny, but nor did they wish to glorify an avaricious and arbitrary king. This problem of balance quickly becomes apparent in the work of Polydore Vergil, an Italian scholar who was commissioned by Henry VII around 1506 to write a history of England. In crafting his history, Polydore Vergil found it insufficient to rely on the interpretations of later medieval English chronicles alone. Following the humanist ideal of criticism, Vergil sought out the earliest sources he could find, such as the works of Tacitus, Gildas and Bede.[5] Although he mercilessly picked apart even the legends of Brutus the Trojan and King Arthur, when Vergil's account reached the events of the fifteenth century, the critical lens slipped away and there was a clear bias in favour of Henry VII and the Tudors. Many of the events in the reign of Henry VII were attributed to divine providence or the whims of *fortuna*, causative explanations that he had disdained for earlier periods.[6] Even when Vergil acknowledged Henry's shortcomings as a monarch and the disgruntlement of his people, it was always because the king was "blighted by ill-fortune."[7] In comparison, Vergil's treatment of Cardinal Wolsey, in later editions of the *Historia*, placed the blame for the Cardinal's actions

---

[4] Polydore Vergil, *The Anglica Historia of Polydore Vergil A.D. 1485-1537,* trans. Denys Hay (London: Camden Series, Vol. LXXIV, 1950), xxix

[5] Ibid.

[6] Vergil, *The Anglica Historia of Polydore Vergil*, 127.

[7] Ibid.

firmly in his own hands rather than placing him at the mercy of the capricious Lady Fortune.[8]

What is even more striking in analyzing Vergil's *Historia* are the numerous deletions of politically sensitive material from the 1534 printed edition that are present in the earlier manuscript. Twenty years elapsed between the completion of the manuscript (1513) and the printing of the 1534 edition, a delay that Denys Hay has attributed to Vergil's anxieties about the political climate of Henry VIII's court.[9] Polydore Vergil had a special copy of the manuscript commissioned for Henry VIII, but for reasons unknown it was never presented to the king.[10] It is probable that given Henry's increasing concerns over producing an heir to his throne, as well as his break with the Roman Catholic Church in the 1530s, Vergil felt internal pressure to bury details that would embarrass the crown for fear of incurring the wrath of the king.

Thomas More harboured anxieties that were similar to those expressed by Vergil and these anxieties certainly influenced his works. Several of More's biographers have gone into great depth about his distaste for tyranny and his worry that it might once again become a reality in his beloved England; these worries gave birth to several of his works on the subject, including *The History of Richard III* and *Utopia*.[11] Given More's family ties to theatre as well as his own attempts at writing drama, the many scholars of the dramatic arts have argued that *Richard III* is history with dramatic flair.[12] While one expects More to juxtapose tyranny and virtue through his characters of Richard III and Edward IV, there is no true "righteous king" in the history. More uses irony to portray Edward IV as a usurper who is only redeemed through the practice of good government. Paradoxically, the only other logical candidate to play Richard III's antithesis was Henry VII, More's most recent example of tyranny; the work, however, was never finished and thus Henry does not appear, as he does in Shakespeare's play, to defeat the tyrant in the end. More uses Edward to warn his readers about the dangers of ruling selfishly and turning one's back on the laws of the realm, which the real Henry VII was guilty of in the latter years of his

---

[8] Vergil, *The Anglica Historia of Polydore Vergil*, 257.

[9] Vergil, *The Anglica Historia of Polydore Vergil*, xiv-xvi.

[10] Ibid.

[11] Betteridge, *Writing Faith and Telling Tales*; R.W. Chambers, *The Saga and Myth of Sir Thomas More*, (London: British Academy, 1926); Fox, *Politics and Literature*; Richard Marius, *Thomas More*, (New York: Knopf; Distributed by Random House, 1984).

[12] Leonard F. Dean, "Literary Problems in More's Richard III," *Modern Language Association* 58, no. 1 (1943); Arthur Noel Kincaid, "The Dramatic Structure of Sir Thomas More's History of King Richard III," *Studies in English Literature, 1500-1900* 12, no. 2 (1972); A.F. Pollard, "The Making of Sir Thomas More's Richard III," In *Historical Essays in Honor of James Tait*, ed. J.G. Edwards, V.H. Galbraith and E.F. Jacobs, (Manchester: Printed for Subscribers, 1933).

reign. In order to grapple with the tyranny of the past and the possibility of its existence in the future, More infused *Richard III* with irony and there exists many parallels between the character of Edward IV and the real life Henry VII that make a case for the former standing as a proxy for the first Tudor king. With the tyrant Richard serving as an effective distraction, it was far less precarious for More to criticize the previous regime, especially through the guise of a fictionalized Edward IV.

Similar devices can also be found when examining More's *Utopia,* a two-book humanist treatise on the fictional island of Utopia and its people and customs. Book one outlines a fictitious conversation between More and a Portuguese sailor named Raphael Hythloday on various aspects of English policy. In book two More gives a detailed account, through Hythloday, of the various Utopian policies and customs. Although More's conclusion to *Utopia* insists that Hythloday is a real person, this claim is clearly tongue in cheek.[13] Raphael Hythloday's last name translates from Greek as "peddler of nonsense" and More was assuming that his target readership, mostly consisting of other scholars, would pick up on this and understand the irony of his truth claims.[14] More placed into Hythloday's mouth his own critiques of England's existing social order, making very clear his aversion to kings and their courts through discussion of their cruelty and avarice.[15] More also made use of a fictionalized John Morton, cardinal archbishop of Canterbury (d. 1500), who served in real life as Henry VII's most trusted counselor and in whose household More served as a young adolescent. In *Utopia,* Morton acts as a facilitator for Hythloday's criticisms of Tudor England and actively engages with many of his ideas. In this way, More could discreetly voice his concerns about tyranny (including that of Henry VII) without incurring the wrath of Henry VIII. This is especially significant since at the time, More was considering whether to enter into the service of the English crown and the spotlight under which he found himself meant that he had to be careful.[16]

This thesis will explore the links between the political climate of Henry VIII's court and the choices that contemporary writers and scholars made in creating and publishing their representations of the early Tudors. Ultimately, it was fear and pressure that ensured that Polydore Vergil and Sir Thomas More altered their narratives and refrained from making any

---

[13] Thomas More, "Utopia," in *The Complete Works of Sir Thomas More, Vol. 4,* ed. Edward Surtz, J.H. Hexter (New Haven; London: Yale University Press, 1965), 137-140.

[14] Betteridge, *Writing Faith and Telling Tales,* 82.

[15] Betteridge, *Writing Faith and Telling Tales,* 82-84.

[16] Marius, *Thomas More,* 191.

open accusations of tyranny towards Henry VII and Henry VIII. In both cases, patronage played a large role in shaping the creation of these historical representations so that the work reflected the wishes of the patron. That the "Tudor myth" continues to be a popular narrative to this day indicates the power of historical interpretation and the extensive role of these narratives in the negotiation and consolidation of royal power.

Chapter 1: The Wars of the Roses and the Rise of the Tudors

From 1455 to 1485, much of England's nobility was consumed by a series of dynastic conflicts for the English throne now known as the Wars of the Roses. These conflicts were dubbed "the Cousins' Wars" because they were fought between two rival branches of the Plantagenet family, the houses of York and Lancaster.[17] When the Lancaster claimants fell in battle, Henry Tudor saw a chance to claim the throne and emerged as a leader, rallying Lancastrian supporters to his banner against the Yorkists and their king, Richard III. Henry's claim to the Lancastrian dynastic inheritance was problematic on two counts: first, it was through his mother, Margaret (and thus the female line), and second, her Plantagenet descent was through the Beauforts, an illegitimate branch of the Plantagenets barred from the line of succession.[18] As a descendant from this line, Henry Tudor should have been excluded from the list of potential heirs to the throne.[19] In addition, Henry also made another oblique dynastic claim: Henry VII's father, Edmund, was the son of Owen Tudor and Catherine of Valois, the queen consort of England and mother to the Lancastrian king Henry VI.[20] Although Henry VII repeatedly invoked this close family relationship as a basis for the legitimacy of his reign, it did not give him any technical claim to the throne. To remedy this, after Bosworth he married Edward IV's daughter, Elizabeth of York, to bolster his claim.[21] Henry further portrayed himself as the king who ended the Wars of the Roses by uniting the warring factions through this marriage to a Yorkist princess.[22] When he took the throne, Henry VII and his agents worked assiduously to ensure that the king's claim appeared legitimate, because the claims that he made through lineage were tenuous at best.

In an attempt to consolidate his power and undermine the cause of those who would challenge him, Henry VII and his agents projected his reign and his union with Elizabeth as the end of the Wars of the Roses. After decades of fighting between two of England's noble houses and the virtual eradication of Lancastrian leadership, the realm was ready for the cessation of

---

[17] Christine Carpenter, *The Wars of the Roses: politics and the constitution in England c. 1437-1509*, (Cambridge; New York: Cambridge University Press, 1997).

[18] Chrimes, *Henry VII,* 50; Cunningham, *Henry VII*, 10-11.

[19] Chrimes, *Henry VII,* 49, Cunningham, *Henry VII*, 10-12; Vergil, *The Anglica Historia of Polydore Vergil,* 7, 5.

[20] Please see Fig. 1 for a diagram of the descendants of Edward III, 69

[21] Chrimes, "Accession, Coronation, Marriage, and Family," in *Henry VII,* 50-67.

[22] Ibid.

hostilities and Henry was presented as a king who would bring peace to his people.[23] Henry had not only claimed the realm by right of conquest, he also claimed legitimacy through his uncle, former Lancastrian king Henry VI. In order to cement and emphasize this claim, Henry VII spent much of his reign organizing for the canonization of his uncle – a project that was only abandoned under Henry VIII after England's break with Rome in the 1530s.[24] As will be explored at more length below, as part of the campaign to solidify his claim to the throne and win the support of the English and Welsh people, Henry VII also traced his lineage back to ancient British and Welsh kings Arthur and Cadwallader.[25] This painted his reign as the culmination of centuries-old prophecies as well as the will of God. He placed further emphasis on his connection with the kings of old when he named his firstborn son after king Arthur in 1486.[26]

Anxious to immortalize his reign in the eyes of his people, Henry VII commissioned Polydore Vergil, a prominent Italian scholar, to write a history of England that favoured the Tudors and placed them on equal footing with the great English kings of the past. Vergil, who was renowned for widely circulated works such as *Adagia* and *De Inventoribus Rerum*, enjoyed friendships and correspondences with many influential scholars throughout Europe and it was this reputation among the scholars and courts of Europe that Henry VII was hoping to exploit when he commissioned the Latin *Anglica Historia*. The goal was for a history that was favourable to the Tudors to transcend the borders of England and to be disseminated across Europe; the king also hoped to send a clear message to other European monarchs about the strength of his claim.[27] Henry's patronage of Polydore Vergil was part of a campaign that extended patronage to many other European humanists, including Bernard André, Baldassare Castiglione, and Desiderius Erasmus.[28]

Henry VII's desire to project a favourable image of his rule throughout Europe was jeopardized by challenges to his reign.[29] The first threat to Henry's throne was Edward, earl of

---

[23] Chrimes, *Henry VII*, 64-67; Cunningham, *Henry VII*, 49.

[24] Sharpe, *Selling the Tudor Monarchy*, 84; Denys Hay, *Polydore Vergil: Renaissance Historian and Man of Letters*, (Oxford: Clarendon Press, 1952),110-122.

[25] Howard Dobin, *Merlin's Disciples: Prophecy, Poetry and Power in Renaissance England*, (Stanford: Stanford University Press, 1990), 51.

[26] Chrimes, *Henry VII*, 66-67, Cunningham, *Henry VII*, 54; Jonathan Hughes, *Arthurian Myths and Alchemy: The Kingship of Edward IV*, (Pheonix Mill: Sutton Publishing Limited, 2002), 307.

[27] Fox, *Politics and Literature*, 17.

[28] Fox, *Politics and Literature*, 15-17.

[29] Sharpe, *Selling the Tudor Monarchy*, 61-80.

Warwick, the only son and heir of George, duke of Clarence. As Edward IV's nephew, the young earl of Warwick held an arguably better claim to the throne than Henry VII and posed a direct challenge to his rule. Perceiving the threat to his crown, Henry VII was quick to imprison Edward in the Tower of London in 1485, where he was not seen again for two years.[30] Furthermore, the disappearance of Edward IV's heirs in the Tower of London was also shrouded in mystery. After being imprisoned in 1483 by their uncle, Richard III, the young princes were most likely killed, but their demise was not proven and some harboured hopes that they were still alive well into Henry VII's reign.[31] The lack of clarity about the whereabouts of the earl of Warwick, as well as the mysterious fate of his cousins, proved fertile ground for pretense and speculation. The potential existence of three Plantagenet heirs proved a rallying point for Henry VII's opponents. As impostors and pretenders to the throne emerged in the early years of Henry's reign, disgruntled Yorkists rallied their support against him.

In 1487, the earl of Warwick made his first appearance in two years when he was presented in front of St. Paul's to expose the pretender Lambert Simnel, who claimed to be the earl of Warwick.[32] Many powerful members of the nobility had thrown their support behind Simnel, including Margaret of York, dowager duchess of Burgundy and sister of Edward IV, Richard III, and the duke of Clarence. Simnel and his supporters invaded England in 1487 with a force to be reckoned with, but the king was well prepared and his forces defeated Simnel at the Battle of Stoke.[33] According to Polydore Vergil, Simnel was graciously spared by the king and put to service in the scullery and later on as a falconer.[34] This would not be Henry's last brush with pretenders to the throne of England. In 1491, Perkin Warbeck rose up as a leader for the Yorkists when he assumed the identity of Richard of York, the second son of Edward IV and one of the missing princes in the Tower.[35] Just as Simnel had found support among high profile proponents of the Yorkist cause, Warbeck soon counted the earl of Desmond and (again)

---

[30] Christine Carpenter, "Edward, styled earl of Warwick (1475–1499)", *Oxford Dictionary of National Biography*, Oxford University Press, 2004; online edn, Jan 2008 [http://0-www.oxforddnb.com.mercury.concordia.ca/view/article/8525, accessed 8 March 2016].

[31] Rosemary Horrox, "Edward V (1470–1483)", *Oxford Dictionary of National Biography*, Oxford University Press, 2004; online edn, Sept 2013 [http://0-www.oxforddnb.com.mercury.concordia.ca/view/article/8521, accessed 8 March 2016].

[32] Carpenter, "Edward, styled earl of Warwick (1475–1499)".

[33] Cunningham, *Henry VII*, 54-58.

[34] Vergil, *The Anglica Historia of Polydore Vergil*, 25.

[35] Cunningham, *Henry VII*, 65; Chrimes, *Henry VII*, 69-70.

Margaret of York as his allies. However, his greatest support came from Charles VIII, king of France, who hoped to distract Henry VII from French annexation of Brittany.[36] For several years, Warbeck faced challenges to his claims, but his cause rapidly found support in 1497 after Henry VII's heavy taxation sparked rebellion in Cornwall. In September of that year, Warbeck arrived in England and engaged with the royal forces in Exeter before he was captured in 1498. This time, the king was less merciful and after confessing that he was not Richard Plantagenet, in 1499 Warbeck was hanged at Tyburn.[37] Edward, earl of Warwick, who had been in the Tower continuously from 1485, was executed at the same time as Warbeck.[38]

The later years of Henry VII's reign marked both a decline in the king's health and, in the eyes of many of his subjects, his character. As expressed by Sean Cunningham in his recent biography of Henry VII, "dynastic insecurity soon overrode the promotion of balanced and indifferent rule."[39] With the help of his counselors, Richard Empson and Edmund Dudley, the king expanded his landed estate until it yielded nearly double the income of Richard III's estate.[40] Under Henry, the clergy was more heavily taxed than under any regime in the past, and he exploited his feudal rights over those who held land from him by selling off the wardships of underage heirs and the marriages of his tenants' widows. He charged livery fees to those who inherited estates and made it very clear that those who attempted to avoid these fees would be subject to harsh financial penalty.[41] Landholders and aristocrats, who had traditionally acted as king's councillors and projected his power across the kingdom, were increasingly being passed up in favour of lawyers, judges and other professionals who could help Henry bypass administrative structures through "legal trickery." As Cunningham has put it, this was "council with very little apparent counsel."[42] As the landed gentry and magnates of the realm were increasingly alienated from the administration of the regime, Henry issued thousands of bonds to enforce their loyalty to the crown. In turn, their acceptance of the king's right to demand payment

---

[36] Cunningham, *Henry VII*, 67-8.

[37] Cunningham, *Henry VII*, 97; Chrimes, *Henry VII*, 93.

[38] Carpenter, "Edward, styled earl of Warwick (1475–1499)".

[39] Cunningham, *Henry VII*, 123.

[40] S. J. Gunn, "Henry VII (1457–1509)", *Oxford Dictionary of National Biography*, Oxford University Press, 2004; online edn, Jan 2008 [http://0-www.oxforddnb.com.mercury.concordia.ca/view/article/12954, accessed 19 Jan 2016]; Cunningham, *Henry VII*, 132-133.

[41] Gunn, 'Henry VII (1457–1509)'; Cunningham, *Henry VII*, 132-133.

[42] Cunningham, *Henry VII*, 126.

served to reinforce Henry's authority over the magnates of the realm.[43] By Henry's last years, Empson and Dudley had earned a reputation for their ruthlessness in filling the royal coffers. As they enforced the policies of the king, every source of income was "being squeezed hard, and others less reputable, such as the sale of office and even the sale of the king's favour in lawsuits, were being added to them."[44]

Like his father, Henry VIII faced his own challenges as the heir to a dynasty that had its share of opponents. Henry VIII's insecurities about possibly having to face these challenges himself led the young king to distance his reign from that of his father's.[45] Upon his accession, Henry VIII had Richard Empson and Edmund Dudley arrested to send a message that he was cutting ties with the past. They were subsequently tried for treason and brutally executed for the public to bear witness.[46] Under the previous regime, Dudley and Empson ran a corrupt justice system and, as a result, there was no true way to tell if any of those convicted under Henry VII were given a fair trial.[47] In response to this quandary Henry VIII issued a general pardon as one of his first acts as king of England. This pardon exonerated all those sentenced for crimes ranging from petty theft to high treason.[48]

As a young man, Henry VIII was described by many as a temperate, handsome, athletic and charismatic individual; a true opposite of the reputation he would earn in the later years of his life.[49] Venetian diplomat Pietro Pasqualigo, was so impressed by the young king that he wrote home on 4 April 1515 with a very flattering description of Henry, who was just two months shy of his twenty-fifth birthday. "The king is the handsomest potentate I ever set eyes on," he wrote, praising the king as an accomplished ruler who could speak French, English, Latin and "a little Italian."[50] The main texts under consideration in the pages that follow were written first in the 1510s (with Vergil's *Historia* undergoing significant revisions in the 1530s). Henry's first decade of rule was marked by a number of crises and challenges. The king undertook an aggressive war

---

[43] Cunningham, *Henry VII*, 127-128.

[44] Cunningham, *Henry VII*, 135-142; Gunn, "Henry VII (1457–1509)".

[45] J.J. Scarisbrick, "The Renewal of the Hundred Years War," in *Henry VIII*, (London: Eyre & Spottiswoode, 1968), 21-40.

[46] Sharpe, *Selling the Tudor Monarchy*, 69.

[47] Scarisbrick, *Henry VIII*, 10-11.

[48] "Henry VIII: Pardon Roll, Part 1", in *Letters and Papers, Foreign and Domestic, Henry VIII, Volume 1, 1509-1514*, ed. J S Brewer (London, 1920), pp. 203-216 http://www.british-history.ac.uk/letters-papers-hen8/vol1/pp203-216 [accessed 19 January 2015].

[49] Scarisbrick, *Henry VIII*, 15-17.

[50] Ibid.

policy by reviving the conflict with France, which was fought intermittently between 1513 and 1521. The first year of Henry's war with France was wrought with failed campaigns that drained the royal coffers and with Henry's attention fixated across the channel, England was left vulnerable to attack from the Scots. The Scottish king chose the fall of 1513 to strike from the north while the Henry was away.[51] At the battle of Flodden, the Scots were handed a resounding defeat under the regency of Catherine of Aragon and the military leadership of the Earl of Surrey.[52] Despite initial failures in his war with France, Henry also found some success on the battlefield. Following his 1513 campaign in France, Henry returned triumphantly to England fresh off his victories at the Battle of the Spurs in August and the siege of Tournai in September.[53] In the early years of England's renewed conflicts with France, Cardinal Thomas Wolsey rose to power in a secular position at the royal court. Wolsey became Henry VIII's trusted counselor and served as Lord Chancellor from 1515 to 1529.[54] In the 1510s, Henry was largely uninterested in the administrative duties adorning his crown and Wolsey was reported to have taken over many of the affairs of the realm for the king.[55] From 1511-13, England was plunged into economic crisis after a series of bad harvests. These were compounded by wheat crop failures in 1519-21 and 1527-29, creating food shortages, which were especially devastating after the rise in England's population over recent years.[56] Along with England's economic crises, Henry also had to contend with the rise and spread of Lutheranism in the 1520s. With the help of Cardinal Wolsey, the crown employed stricter measures to fight heretics in England, including book burnings and heresy trials.[57] The king's hopes were that the fight against heretics would see his people unite under his rule against a common enemy and distract the populace from his growing dynastic insecurities.[58] These anxieties would later be exacerbated by the king's inability to produce an heir.[59]

---

[51] Scarisbrick, *Henry VIII*, 38.

[52] Ibid.

[53] Scarisbrick, *Henry VIII*, 36-38.

[54] Scarisbrick, *Henry VIII*, 42.

[55] Peter Gwyn, *The King's Cardinal: The Rise and Fall of Thomas Wolsey*, (London: Barrie & Jenkins, 1990), 207-209.

[56] Gwyn, *The King's Cardinal*, 422-423.

[57] Gwyn, *The King's Cardinal*, 481-90.

[58] E. W. Ives, "Henry VIII (1491–1547)", *Oxford Dictionary of National Biography*, Oxford University Press, 2004; online edn, May 2009 [http://0-www.oxforddnb.com.mercury.concordia.ca/view/article/12955, accessed 19 Jan 2015].

[59] Ibid.

Chapter 2: English Historical Writing and the Advent of Humanism in the 15th and 16th centuries

Among the instruments through which monarchical authority was negotiated and understood were humanist political histories and chronicles. Henry VII and Henry VIII sought to manage the diffusion of the royal image through an elaborate propaganda campaign to ensure the approval and cooperation of their subjects. Artists and men of letters from all over Europe became an integral part of the campaign to amplify the magnificence of Tudor rule. As sixteenth-century chronicler Edward Hall has suggested, kings and princes owed a great debt to historians, for without them monarchs could not hope to achieve eternal fame and "suppress that deadly beast oblivion."[60] The Tudor patronage system helped to spawn a new generation of history writing in England, which immortalized the Tudors as well as English kings of the past – famous and infamous. We must look now to the scholarship surrounding the evolution of English historiography and the contributions of some of its most significant actors.

While historians generally agree that the writing of history in England was markedly different after the decline of the Latin monastic chronicle, there is a fierce debate as to whether changes over two centuries in England's vernacular writing culture can account for this transformation, or whether the exogenous intervention of the Italian humanists was indispensible to this process. Some historians, especially those writing in the 1960s and earlier, have tended to see a dichotomy between English native intellectual culture and a "new" and entirely Italian humanist method brought by scholars such as Polydore Vergil to Northern Europe in the 1500s. This chasm within the scholarship of English historical writing is clearly displayed in a debate between historians F.J. Levy and May McKisack, whose surveys on Tudor historiography were published four years apart. Both scholars adopted polarizing stances on the evolution of history writing in sixteenth-century England and the decline of the chronicle. Levy's book *Tudor Historical Thought*, published in 1967, is often regarded as the first full scale survey of Tudor historiography. His work argues that by the fifteenth century, "the art of writing [Latin] chronicles had nearly vanished," and that the advent of humanism was the most important factor

---

[60] Edward Hall, *The Union of Two Noble and Illustre Famelies of Lancastre & Yorke*, (London: G. Woodfall, 1809), 1.

in this disappearance.[61] London civic chroniclers of late sixteenth century, such as Edward Hall

and Richard Grafton, are regarded as successors to the Italian man of letters, Polydore Vergil, and

are reputed to have borrowed from his work extensively. Although many scholars of the Italian

Renaissance would agree with Levy's affirmation that "the original stock of the plant was Italian,

and to understand what happened in the England of Thomas More it is necessary to visit the Italy

of Petrarch,"[62] other scholars of English historiography, such as May McKisack, would argue that

the celebrated critical ethos of the Tudor period was active before the intervention of humanism.

McKisack ends the introduction to her book, *Medieval History in the Tudor Age*, with an

acknowledgement of the publication of Levy's book a few years before the completion of her

own work. Here she expressed hope that "there is room for more than one approach in the

historical and antiquarian activities of the Tudor age."[63] McKisack argued that although Polydore

Vergil is credited with introducing the spirit of historical criticism into Tudor historiography, the

work of sixteenth-century chronicler John Rastell would suggest otherwise. She asserts that

Rastell, a lawyer, printer and brother-in-law to Thomas More, was a successor to one of the great

London chroniclers, Robert Fabyan, and that his 1529 *Pastyme of the People* "affords clear

evidence that the spirit of historical criticism, most commonly associated with Polydore Vergil,

was already active in a native author."[64] Alternatively, Levy's work asserts that Rastell was well

acquainted with Vergil.[65] According to Levy, Rastell's *Pastyme* "seems to owe something to

Polydore, frequently in method, sometimes in particular opinions," and that there was no

"inherent improbability" in Rastell having become acquainted with Vergil through their mutual

connection, Thomas More.[66] May McKisack's work directly takes issue with such an

interpretation as she included a footnote disputing Levy's claim that Rastell and Vergil were

acquainted with one other. Eric W. Cochrane's *Historians and Historiography in the Italian

Renaissance* in 1980 demonstrates that this split within the scholarship over the influence of

humanism on northern intellectual currents continued a decade after the works of McKisack and

Levy. The evolution of history writing in England is something that Cochrane attributes to

---

[61] F.J. Levy, *Tudor Historical Thought* (San Marino: The Huntington Library, 1967), 9, 24.

[62] Levy, *Tudor Historical Thought*, 33.

[63] May McKisack, "Introduction," in *Medieval History in the Tudor Age* (Oxford: Clarendon Press, 1971), vii.

[64] McKisack, *Medieval History in the Tudor Age*, 98.

[65] Ibid.

[66] Levy, *Tudor Historical Thought*, 72-73.

Polydore Vergil and his *Anglica Historia.* Cochrane argues that Vergil, as well as other Italian humanists who ventured abroad, "succeeded in imposing history upon cultures that had previously known only chronicles."[67] Such a view does not take into account that the vernacular civic chronicles in England were certainly a precursor to the works of historians such as Thomas More and Edward Hall.[68] Nor does it acknowledge that the influence of native traditions was by no means incompatible with the adoption of humanist principles by these historians.

Mark Salber Phillips' recent monograph, *On Historical Distance,* explores the profound effect of humanist traditions on the writing of history in a European context and discusses how the prejudices with which humanists viewed their medieval predecessors continue to resurface in the present day.[69] This, he argues, discourages the modern-day historian from looking at chronicles as a rich historical genre with vivid traditions of its own.[70] Instead, we regard chronicles as bland, colourless records of the past that simply enumerate facts in a chronological sequence.[71] Phillips's work draws on decades of medievalist scholarship on the evolution of the chronicle form, His approach makes a case for the influence of humanism while simultaneously refusing to dismiss the integral role assumed by medieval chroniclers in the evolution of European historiography. This trend within the scholarship of the last three decades effectively marries the two traditions in a way that acknowledges the influence of foreigners like Polydore Vergil on English history writing as well as the ability of his successors in England to make it their own.

Most scholarship since the 1960s has tended to caution against viewing the development of humanism in northern Europe as merely a product of the import of renewed Italian culture. This is a more balanced view which gives much of the credit to Italian scholars, but does not ignore the existence of a large web of ideas that involved and enveloped Europe as a whole. Such a stance sketches the spread of humanism in Italy, Northern Europe and England as the culmination of centuries of trade in ideas and knowledge, while doing away with the problematic dichotomy of medieval versus modern histories. The "northern" variant of humanism was both in

---

[67] Eric Cochrane, *Historians and Historiography in the Italian Renaissance,* (Chicago: The University of Chicago Press, 1981), 348.

[68] Malcolm Richardson, *Middle-Class Writing in Late Medieval London* (London: Pickering & Chatto, 2011), 20; Fox, *Politics and Literature,* 228-229.

[69] Phillips, *On Historical Distance,* 22.

[70] Ibid.

[71] Phillips, *On Historical Distance,* 22.

continual contact with Italian developments through travel, correspondence, and writings, and at the same time developed in ways that reflected local traditions and interests. For instance, a number of Italian scholars came to teach at Oxford and Cambridge in the later years of the fifteenth century, while thousands from France, England and Germany also went to pursue their studies at Italian universities throughout the middle ages.[72] Many of these scholars would return home to teach at their native universities after completing their studies, thus bringing with them the wealth of knowledge and ideas they had acquired abroad from the Italian scholars.[73] This was a relationship of give, take and exchange, which actually rendered Italian and northern humanism separate currents in their own right with some distinct local features. In his 1989 survey of Tudor historiography, Alistair Fox acknowledged the effects of this exchange of ideas on scholarship throughout Europe in his discussion of Desiderius Erasmus. Fox argues that it was the humanists in London, such as Thomas More and John Colet, who first took Erasmus seriously. He influenced them and in turn, they influenced him – particularly Colet. Like many scholars before him, Erasmus traveled to Italy and, according to Fox, "it was the fact of returning to this English ambience" and "bringing with him the fruits of his Italian experience" that inspired the writing of his most famous work, *The Praise of Folly*.[74] In a similar vein, Fox argued that Thomas More's *History of Richard III* was profoundly influenced by Polydore Vergil's *Anglica Historia*. Fox supported this through a comparison of several passages from both works. Here he argued that the orations of *Anglica Historia* are closely paralleled in More's work, where "in the description of Richard III, [he] duplicates the sequence of details incorporated in Vergil's portrait almost exactly."[75] Just as Erasmus drew inspiration from intellectual currents all over Europe, Thomas More was similarly influenced by a network of European humanist scholars, which included Polydore Vergil.

Mary-Rose McLaren's 2002 study on the London chronicles of the fifteenth century represents a facet of the newer scholarship on English history writing which acknowledges that medieval and Renaissance intellectual cultures were not mutually exclusive. Her work argues that by the fifteenth century the medieval Latin monastic chronicle was making way for the city

---

[72] Quentin Skinner, *The Foundations of Modern Political Thought* Vol 1 (Cambridge: Cambridge University Press, 1978), 194-198.

[73] Skinner, *The Foundations of Modern Political Thought*, 197.

[74] Fox, *Politics and Literature*, 78.

[75] Fox, *Politics and Literature*, 117.

chronicle.[76] This tradition, which saw it earliest development in London, was the first attempt by ordinary laypeople to write their own histories and they reveal "a self-conscious attempt by Londoners to record events and their meanings."[77] These accounts were the products of London's citizen merchants, who may or may not have been involved in civic government.[78] McLaren interestingly argues that the city chronicles reveal a "vibrant, literate, intellectual life amongst the lay citizens of London" that challenges many of the previous ideas of what medieval English society was like. London's chroniclers were not merely waiting for the humanists of Italy to pull them out of their primitive ways; they were part of a tradition of history writing that had evolved in its own right. They paved the way for the writing of critical, national histories of England that would become a staple of the Tudor period.[79]

Similarly to McLaren, Malcolm Richardson has recently argued that "middle-class" writing in England emerged as a result of a writing culture that had existed since the 1350s. There was a tendency in previous scholarship of the 1980s to speculate about the revolutionary effects of print on intellectual and social history, but as Richardson puts it, "cooler heads" eventually realized that cause and effect were more complicated, and "while print unquestionably had large effects on the circulation of ideas and general ability to read, the need for the printing press was the result of an existing western European culture of reading."[80] Richardson's *Middle-Class Writing in Late Medieval London* (2010) asserts that the mercantile class of London inadvertently helped create practices of writing, record keeping and research among England's urban elite. The literate practices of the mercantile class also included editing and the ability to critically examine texts. These practices created "habits of using texts" which in turn provided humanists in England with useful ways of thinking about them.[81] "It is therefore no accident," argues Richardson that "many early English humanists were born into the guild culture," and that traces of mercantile writing practices can be found in the works of "children of the middle class," such as Thomas More and Edward Hall. In a similar fashion, Thomas Betteridge's 2013 study on the works of Thomas More displays very effectively that city chronicles and humanist histories were

---

[76] Mary-Rose McLaren, *The London Chronicles of the Fifteenth Century: a Revolution in English Writing* (Cambridge: D.S. Brewer, 2002), 3.

[77] Ibid.

[78] McLaren, *The London Chronicles*, 3-13.

[79] McLaren, *The London Chronicles*, 3, 48.

[80] Richardson, *Middle-Class Writing*, 4.

[81] Richardson, *Middle-Class Writing*, 171.

not mutually exclusive. More's works, like those of John Leland and Geoffrey Chaucer, could invoke the "sense of [the English language], as, at its best, confirming classical Christian learning with popular sayings, fables, and tales to create an authoritative ethical language."[82] According to Betteridge, More belonged to the tradition of vernacular English writing just as much as he belonged to the tradition of Latin humanist scholarship.[83]

Having evolved from the Levy-McKisack debate of the late 1960s and early 70s, the newer scholarship on the transformation of history writing in fifteenth- and sixteenth-century England allows us to come full circle. Just as Thomas More was influenced by other humanist scholars outside of England, John Rastell was not exclusively a successor to the London Chronicle tradition, nor was he merely emulating the Italian humanists. While his *Pastyme of the People* reflected peculiarly English concerns and contexts, the newer scholarship allows one to argue *both* for Rastell's immersion in an English intellectual culture that was already part of larger European intellectual currents, as well as for the direct influence of Polydore Vergil, and other humanists, on his work. Newer trends in the scholarship of English history writing have become less concerned with separating the medieval chronicle from Renaissance humanist history, and effectively recognizes that it is impossible to do so. Both chroniclers and humanists were mutually influential in the evolution of historical writing throughout Europe - it does not (and should not) have to be a question of one tradition eliminating the other.

That there is no absolute distinction between the chronicle form and the humanist political history also begs a clarification of what exactly the terms "history" or "historian" mean in the context of Tudor England. The works of both medievalist and early modern scholars define the purpose of history in the sixteenth century as instructional and entertaining.[84] Mary-Rose McLaren writes that the civic chronicles were carefully crafted narratives in which historical events were placed in patterns that would convey meaning to the reader or serve as a subtle contemporary commentary. The civic chroniclers also made use of devices such as juxtaposition, allegories and irony to achieve this in the hopes that they could impart a moral truth to their readers.[85] The humanists of early modern Europe made use of similar devices in crafting their narratives and representations of the past. Mark Salber Phillips's work on Francesco Guicciardini

---

[82] Richardson, *Middle-Class Writing,* 171.

[83] Betteridge, *Writing Faith and Telling Tales,* 8-9.

[84] Phillips, *On Historical Distance,* 26; Antonia Gransden, *Historical Writing in England vol. 2: c. 1307 to the Early Sixteenth Century,* (London: Routledge and Kegan Paul, 1974), 459-460.

[85] McLaren, *The London Chronicles,* 50, 95, 97.

and Niccòlo Macchiavelli also reveals that the humanists shared the chroniclers' motives for writing about the past. Humanists believed that to record the evil and virtuous deeds of historical persons could impart wisdom to the reader and guide them to virtue. History could serve as an example of virtuous behaviour while also providing a cautionary tale of what might happen should the mistakes of the past be repeated. [86] Daniel Woolf's *Reading History in Early Modern England* also corroborates this idea from the perspective of the sixteenth-century reader. The work asserts that people read histories for much the same reasons that they were composed: for entertainment and instruction. Historically-themed works also served as a way for readers to become informed about their milieus; like the chroniclers, humanists also used the past to make commentaries on contemporary events. [87] An interesting component of Woolf's work also explores the consumption of history in the sixteenth century. Here he discusses how chronicles were not necessarily meant to be read in private – most often historical works would have been read aloud in homes and other public spaces. The same is true of humanist writings which were often read out loud (or sung) at the vast majority of courts across the Channel. [88] Thus, not only were these works composed for rhetorical or political purposes, readers were expected to be entertained by them. This accounts for the colourful narrative structure of both chronicles and humanist works, as well as their lack of precision on dates, or accuracy. [89] Vergil's *Historia,* and More's *Richard III* were also written with the entertainment of their readers or audience in mind, thus the narratives progress very much like stories, where empirical precision is not emphasized as it would be in a modern historical work.

An emphasis on entertainment and storytelling places chronicles and humanist works among a wide range of other historically themed genres in Tudor England, such as plays, poems and pageants. While structurally different from the chronicles or humanist political histories, these other genres were created and performed for much the same reasons. Kevin Sharpe's survey of Tudor propaganda discusses the importance of historically themed royal and city pageants under Henry VII and Henry VIII in the negotiation of royal power. [90] For example, the pageant in

---

[86] Mark Salber Phillips, *Francesco Guicciardini: The Historian's Craft* (Toronto: University of Toronto Press, 1977); Phillips, *On Historical Distance*, 44-45.

[87] Daniel Woolf, *Reading History in Early Modern England* (Cambridge: Cambridge University Press, 2000), 130.

[88] Woolf, *Reading History,* 85.

[89] McLaren, *The London Chronicles,* 50-51.

[90] Sharpe, "Performing Supremacy," in *Selling the Tudor Monarchy,* 155-176.

honour of Holy Roman Emperor Charles V's visit to London in the summer of 1522 was organized by the city and featured prominent historical characters such as King Arthur, Alexander the Great and Julius Caesar. The purpose of this was both to associate Henry VIII and the emperor with these powerful figures as well as to disseminate a message of unity and equality between the two sovereigns.[91] McLaren's study of the London chronicles discusses that even the ways in which chroniclers recorded historically themed royal and city pageants was used to instruct the reader or make commentaries about contemporary events or issues that fifteenth and sixteenth-century Londoners were concerned with, such as tyranny.[92] Just as pageants and processions, as well as the way they were recorded, were alive with moral and political meaning, the works of poets and playwrights (who were generally unknown in early Tudor England) were created along historical themes to achieve similar purposes to that of chronicles, and humanist political histories. Historical plays and poems used the past to instruct as well as to entertain readers or audiences. Similarly to sixteenth century chroniclers and humanist scholars, the playwrights and poets of Tudor England made use of a variety of literary devices in the crafting of their narratives, including allegory and irony.[93]

In defining the purpose of "history" in the context of sixteenth-century England, it becomes clear that chronicles and humanist works existed among an assortment of genres of representation that made use of the past to convey a range of meanings and moral truths. These representations also provided a forum through which writers, artists, readers and spectators could comment on contemporary events, engage with the realities of the world they lived in and place themselves within history. That all of these genres were created for similar purposes reveals that "history" in early modern England was a fluid concept and that there was no mould for a "historian" to follow. As such, the historically themed works of chroniclers, playwrights, poets and humanists (such as Polydore Vergil and Thomas More) are not so easily classified or defined. Instead, it is most helpful to consider these works as part of a larger body of historical representations about Tudor England that frequently borrowed from one another in practice and in structure.

---

[91] Sharpe, *Selling the Tudor Monarchy*, 164-165

[92] McLaren, *The London Chronicles*, 51-61.

[93] Sharpe, *Selling the Tudor Monarchy*, 126-127; Betteridge, *Writing Faith and Telling Tales*, 42.

Chapter 3: Polydore Vergil and the *Anglica Historia*

Polydore Vergil was born in Urbino, Italy around the year 1470 and from infancy he was immersed in a tradition of scholarship, which was highly valued by his family. His grandfather taught at the University of Paris and his father enjoyed the patronage of the dukes of Urbino. Vergil was the youngest of four sons and his oldest brother taught philosophy, first at Ferrera and then at Padua, where Polydore Vergil first undertook his studies, following in his brother's footsteps before moving on to study in Bologna.[94] By 20 December 1496, Vergil was ordained as a priest, after which he published two influential books, *Adagia* (1498) and *De inventoribus rerum* (1499), at Urbino. His *Adagia* reached a wide audience throughout Europe and was extremely influential – almost as influential as Desiderius Erasmus' *Adagia,* printed in June 1500. The two scholars put together a collection of proverbs, independently and within two years of each other, leading to a misunderstanding between them as to who had conceived of the idea first.[95] The misunderstanding developed into mutual respect between the two scholars and their friendship can be traced through a series of correspondences. It was through this friendship that Vergil eventually met Thomas More.[96]

In 1502 Vergil was selected by Adriano Castellesi da Corneto, one of Pope Alexander VI's favourites, to travel to England as Castellesi's deputy and agent. Castellesi, who was also an enthusiast of humanist scholarship, had been collector of Peter's pence (a special tax owed to the papacy by the English dating back to the early thirteenth century) since 1490 and Vergil was sent to England as his subcollector. In 1503, Castellesi was elevated to the cardinalship of San Grisogono and Vergil remained in England under his service, retaining the collectorship of Peter's pence. [97] Vergil's impressive career as an established author and representative of humanist learning drew the attention of King Henry VII and it was not long before Vergil was commissioned to write a nationalist "history" of England – one that would glorify the king and his reign. As a result of this commission, Polydore Vergil wrote the *Anglica Historia*, which traced England's past from its Roman heritage to the end of the reign of Henry VII. The *Historia*

---

[94] Hay, *Polydore Vergil*, 1-2.

[95] Hay, *Polydore Vergil*, 22-23.

[96] Ibid.

[97] Hay, *Polydore Vergil*, 1-2.; William J. Connell, "Vergil, Polydore (*c.*1470–1555)", *Oxford Dictionary of National Biography*, Oxford University Press, 2004 [http://0-www.oxforddnb.com.mercury.concordia.ca/view/article/28224, accessed 6 March 2016].

is a work that comprises two volumes with a total of twenty-seven books; one book per reign.[98] A
manuscript of the work, which is now preserved in the Vatican Library, was composed in Latin
and completed in 1513. This version covered events up to 1513. A significantly revised version
of the work that covered events up to 1509 was first printed at Basel in 1534, followed by a
second edition in 1546. For the publication of the 1555 edition of the *Historia,* a twenty-seventh
book covering the reign of Henry VIII up to 1537 was added.[99] For the purpose of this thesis,
Denys Hay's translation and analysis of the *Historia* (1950) will be used in conjunction Sir Henry
Ellis's edition (1844). Hay's edition of the *Historia* covers events from 1485 to 1537, while his
biography of Vergil contains some of the original deleted material, in the form of appendices,
from the Latin manuscript.[100] The Ellis edition of the *Historia* appears in two volumes, covering
Roman Britain to the end of Richard III's reign in 1485.[101] These translations have been
consulted extensively throughout the writing of this project in order to compare the content and
historical interpretations in the Latin manuscript and the printed edition of 1534.

Vergil's accounts of various reigns, including those of Richard III and Henry V, formed
the historical basis of many of Shakespeare's plays. Additionally, scholars in the fields of English
literature and history have been well acquainted with the *Anglica Historia* as a source, yet the
man of letters himself remained an obscure figure until the 1950s. Denys Hay's *Polydore Vergil:
Renaissance Historian and Man of Letters,* published in 1952, was the first survey of Vergil's
works and methodology. In a review of the book, R.D. Richardson expressed surprise that
"Polydore Vergil the man elicited so little recognition until Mr. Hay rescued him from an
illmerited obscurity."[102] Although he begins with an overview of Vergil's life and his most
influential works, Hay is quick to clarify that his purpose is not to create an "exhaustive
consideration of Vergil and his work, still less a 'life and times'."[103] Much of his focus in
Polydore Vergil is on the content, methods and sources of the *Anglica Historia,* though Hay

---

[98] Vergil, *The Anglica Historia of Polydore Vergil,* xv.

[99] Vergil, *The Anglica Historia of Polydore Vergil,* xiii.

[100] Vergil, *The Anglica Historia of Polydore Vergil,* xiii; Hay, *Polydore Vergil,* 199-207.

[101] Polydore Vergil, *Polydore Vergil's English History, From an Early Translation Vol. 1,* ed. Sir Henry
Ellis (London: Camden Society, 1846); Polydore Vergil, *Three Books of Polydore Vergil's English
History Comprising the Reigns of Henry VI, Edward IV, and Richard III,* ed. Sir Henry Ellis, (London:
Camden Society, 1844).

[102] R.D. Richardson, "Review: 'Polydore Vergil, Renaissance Historian and Man of Letters' by Denys
Hay," *Speculum* 28, no. 4 (1953), 892.

[103] Hay, *Polydore Vergil,* x.

admits that this fuller discussion of Vergil's seminal work has resulted in an inadequate discussion as far as his other works, such as the *Adagia*, are concerned.[104] That he chose to focus on the *Anglica Historia* at the expense of Vergil's other works is a result of his belief that it was one of the most important histories of England ever to be published and that it "influenced the treatment of the English past for many generations."[105]

Hay examines Vergil's methodology with admiration, but he seems especially appreciative of Vergil's quest for "truth and objectivity." This portrayal of Vergil is problematic as it imposes a positivist view of historical truth not seen until the 19th century. Recent scholarship, such as the work of Thomas Betteridge, has argued that humanists "believed in the practical application of learning to society," and thus engaged in rigorous source criticism.[106] While humanists actively engaged with classical writings and advocated the return *ad fontes* (original sources), it is "vital to acknowledge the extent to which writers like Chaucer also engaged in a debate with classical writers like Cicero."[107] The search for moral truth was a goal that connected scholars across the centuries, from antiquity into the Renaissance, and the nature of historical knowledge was that it was to be "put into practical moral or political use."[108] Thus, the credibility of a source was essentially determined by its ability to stir the reader towards virtue and convey a desired moral conclusion. Humanism was, as James McConica has expressed, hostile to "abstract speculation"[109] and as a result, Vergil was extremely critical of some of the sources at his disposal. Hay spends a significant portion of his analysis on the Renaissance scholar's broad range of sources for the events prior to 1450 as well as his use of oral history practices for events after 1450.[110] Vergil frequently lamented the absence of adequate documentation as an obstacle throughout the twelve-year project. He did not wish for the *Historia* to be like the traditional annals, but he wished to produce something "polished and refined like the works of classical historians."[111] In a December 1509 letter to king James IV of Scotland, Vergil complained that the Scottish annals were inconsistent, confusing, untrustworthy

---

[104] Hay, *Polydore Vergil*, xii.

[105] Hay, *Polydore Vergil*, vii.

[106] Thomas Betteridge, *Writing Faith and Telling Tales*, 9.

[107] Betteridge, *Writing Faith and Telling Tales*, 53.

[108] Woolf, *Reading History*, 80.

[109] James McConica, "Thomas as Humanist," in *The Cambridge Companion to Thomas More*, ed. George M. Logan (Cambridge: Cambridge University Press, 2011), 23.

[110] Hay, *Polydore Vergil*, 93.

[111] Fox, *Politics and Literature*, 17.

and lacking order.[112] Although he was in the advanced stages of writing the *Historia,* Vergil was uncomfortable with the lack of reliable sources at his disposal when writing about Scotland. "I cannot carry out my plan in strict order," he wrote, "as I know of no author to serve as model."[113] In this letter, he asked James if he could supply him with the annals themselves or "the names of the [Scottish] Kings written in proper order," as well as a list of the king's own illustrious deeds.[114] James IV did not reply to Vergil in person, however the Italian scholar did eventually obtain the information through one of the king's agents who was visiting London some months later.[115]

In his quest to craft a narrative that was unlike the annals, Vergil shuffled out many of the medieval annalists. In discussing pre-Roman Britain, Vergil had to range very widely in his sources, drawing occasionally upon classical writers such as Livy, Eusebius, Halicarnassius and Polybius, in addition to English chroniclers.[116] For Vergil's chapters on Roman Britain, he relied primarily on the works of classical writers, placing great weight on the accounts of Julius Caesar, Tacitus and Suetonius.[117] In discussion of the fall of Roman Britain up to the seventh century, Vergil relied mostly on Gildas, whose *De excidio et conquestu Brittaniae* he discovered and published in 1525.[118] By contrast, in his coverage of events from 800 to 1250, Vergil had a wealth of sources to draw from. He relied a good deal on William of Malmesbury and Matthew Paris, whom he greatly admired and exempted from his general censure of medieval annalists.[119] For this period, Vergil also used Flavio Biondo's works along with Matteo Palmieri's *Prosper of Aquitaine.* From about 1250 to 1350, Ranulf Higden's *Polychronicon* was Vergil's main source, along with a version of the *Brut* chronicle, while the narratives of the fourteenth and fifteenth centuries followed the works of Jean Froissart and Enguerrand de Monstrelet.[120] Many of his sources for this period were printed books, and Hay has suggested that Vergil eagerly watched

---

[112] "Henry VIII: December 1509," in *Letters and Papers, Foreign and Domestic, Henry VIII, Volume 1, 1509-1514,* ed. J S Brewer (London: His Majesty's Stationery Office, 1920), 127-144, accessed February 23, 2016, http://www.british-history.ac.uk/letters-papers-hen8/vol1/pp127-144; Fox, *Politics and Literature,* 17.

[113] G. Gregory Smith, *The Days of James IV 1488-1513: Extracts from the Royal Letters, Polydore Vergil and Hall, Major, Boece, Myln, the State Papers, etc.,* (London: David Nutt, Strand, 1890), 190.

[114] Smith, *The Days of James IV,* 190.

[115] Hay, *Polydore Vergil,* 101.

[116] Hay, *Polydore Vergil,* 86.

[117] Hay, *Polydore Vergil,* 85.

[118] Ibid.

[119] Ibid.

[120] Hay, *Polydore Vergil,* 87.

for new books as they came out to be certain that he was not merely repeating what was already being written.[121] Vergil also sought out his older contemporaries for first hand accounts of the Wars of the Roses, men who were worthy of credit and had been "of importance among royal councilors."[122] Denys Hay comments that it is impossible to know who these sources were with any degree of certainty, however he argues that they may have been advisors to Henry VII who had previously served Edward IV.[123]

According to Hay, Vergil "diligently shuffles out the nonsensical" when his sources conflict. Notably, when coming up against two differing versions of the same event, Vergil had a tendency to simply record both accounts without commenting on them.[124] He does this, for instance, when he discusses the death of Constantine:

> There are somme, which, as concerninge his ende, doe write
> that as hee went owt of Byzantium towardes whote baines for
> the recovery of his helth that hee lefte his mortall life […] but
> there are divers authors, and emonge the rest Sainct Hierom,
> which testifie that he, mindinge to war with the Persians (or,
> as Eutropius saithe, with the Parthians, bie cause thei invaded
> Mesopotamia) did die at a common village, called Aciron, by
> Nicomedia […][125]

This practice seems to have inspired great admiration from Hay, who believes that Vergil "made a virtue of his doubts"; this earned far less sympathy from F.J. Levy.[126] Levy argues that while one of Vergil's legacies was a "heightened sense of criticism," this criticism was "rarely brought to any sort of conclusion."[127] Most of the civic chroniclers of the sixteenth century followed the standard dialectical practice of medieval writing as they recorded all conflicting accounts of an event and very rarely made it clear which account they favoured. Levy argues that the chroniclers adopted these practices due to a "deplorable lack of faith in the new methods of criticism."[128] He further argues that they did not wish to risk that in presenting an opinion or in selecting simply one account they might omit something useful; "The risk was more than most chroniclers dared take, and so they contented themselves by leaving the final choice to the

---

[121] Hay, *Polydore Vergil*, 88.
[122] Hay, *Polydore Vergil*, 78-93, 107.
[123] Hay, *Polydore Vergil*, 93
[124] Hay, *Polydore Vergil*, 107.
[125] Vergil, *Polydore Vergil's English History*, 96-97.
[126] Hay, *Polydore Vergil*, 108.
[127] Levy, *Tudor Historical Thought*, 169.
[128] Ibid.

reader."[129] Alternatively, Alistair Fox argues that this "distinctive feature of the new humanist approach is revealed in Vergil's attempt to control the reader's interpretive response through rhetorical tricks that direct him or her towards the desired moral conclusion."[130] Although Vergil was not explicit about which version of events he thought was correct, this is made very clear by implication even though he opted for the apparent inconclusiveness that Levy finds so frustrating.

Curiously, Vergil was extremely explicit regarding the validity of the legends of Brutus the Trojan - a descendent of Trojan hero Aeneas and the first king of Britain – and those of king Arthur and the prophet Merlin. Though sparse information about the origins of these fabled British kings could be garnered from the *Annales Cambriae*, the *Historia Brittonum*, and the writings of Gildas, the legends gained international interest largely through the popularity of Geoffrey of Monmouth's twelfth century *Historia Regum Britanniae*.[131] Such stories were "firmly embedded in English tradition,"[132] and were appropriated for important political purposes throughout the middle ages and well into the seventeenth century.[133] That these legends were as intricately woven into the fabric of early Britain as the invasion of Julius Caesar meant that it would have been very easy for Vergil to adopt them into his history as fact. However, in his quest to write a historical narrative that marked a departure from the traditional accounts, Vergil "subjects both stories to a devastating historical analysis," as Hay puts it.[134] In particular, he takes issue with Geoffrey of Monmouth's renditions of the popular legends, treating the author with disrespect and rejecting the legends altogether by stating that Geoffrey was giving too much credit to old wives' tales.[135] Here he accuses Geoffrey of "publishing the sowthesaiengs of one Merlin, as prophecies of most assuered and approved trewthe, allways addinge somewhat of his own while he translatethe them into Latine."[136] Some of the criticism that appeared in the manuscript of the *Historia* was softened for the printed versions but for the most part, Vergil

---

[129] Levy, *Tudor Historical Thought*, 169.

[130] Fox, *Politics and Literature*, 111.

[131] J. C. Crick, "Monmouth, Geoffrey of (*d.* 1154/5)", *Oxford Dictionary of National Biography*, Oxford University Press, 2004 [http://0-www.oxforddnb.com.mercury.concordia.ca/view/article/10530, accessed 10 Jan 2016].

[132] Vergil, *The Anglica Historia of Polydore Vergil*, xxix.

[133] Dobin, *Merlin's Disciples*.

[134] Vergil, *The Anglica Historia of Polydore Vergil*, xxix.

[135] Hay, *Polydore Vergil*, 199.

[136] Vergil, *Polydore Vergil's English History*, 29.

remained against the veracity of Geoffrey's account and continued to accuse him of enhancing the stories with "most impudent lyeing".[137]

Vergil's skepticism about the stories of Arthur and Brutus was amplified by his belief that the writers of antiquity were "completely ignorant" of the legends. That the stories rested only on Geoffrey of Monmouth's works was not proof enough for Vergil that Arthur or Brutus had ever been more than tales.[138] Vergil's rejection of the legends ran counter to their already established importance in English kingship and the consolidation of royal power. The Italian scholar held firm to this dismissal -- but only until his narrative reached the events of 1485, when Vergil's attitude towards these stories as they applied to the history of the reign of his first patron, Henry VII, took a significant turn.

From Henry III to Edward IV, English monarchs actively made efforts to trace their lineage back to the great kings of old and Henry VII was no different. This began with William Caxton's printing of Mallory's *Morte d'Arthur* between 1483 and 1485. In Mallory's version of the legend, on the eve of battle with Emperor Lucius, Arthur dreamed of a battle in the sky in which a dragon slays a bear.[139] Jonathan Hughes argues that Caxton cleverly replaced the bear with a boar to reflect Richard's coat of arms as he was anticipating a confrontation between Richard III and Henry Tudor. As a result, the battle of Bosworth was portrayed as the culmination of the prophecy, the battle between Henry and Richard symbolizing the battle between Arthur and his son, Mordred.[140] As though re-enacting the centuries-old prophecy, Henry Tudor, carrying a standard bearing a red dragon, defeated Richard III, whose standard depicted a boar, at Bosworth field and claimed the English crown.[141] Throughout his reign, Henry VII would make efforts to trace his ancestry to king Arthur and Cadwallader, the first king of Britain. After his victory at Bosworth, Henry toured his new kingdom and was received by the city of Worcester in a pageant in 1486. In a poem written to greet him on the occasion of his visit to the city, Henry was hailed as the fulfillment of Cadwallader's prophecy, which foretold that his descendants would one day rule again:

---

[137] Vergil, *Polydore Vergil's English History*, 29.
[138] Hay, *Polydore Vergil*, 110.
[139] Hughes, *Arthurian Myths and Alchemy*, 306.
[140] Ibid.
[141] Hughes, *Arthurian Myths and Alchemy*, 307.

> Cadwaladers Blode lynyally descending, Long hath been
> towalde of such a Prynce coming, Wherfor Frendes, if that I
> shal not lye, This same is the Fulfiller of the Profecye.[142]

Henry Tudor's victory at Bosworth prompted him to elevate Merlin to the place of national prophet, just as the Yorkists and the Lancastrians had done before him during the Wars of the Roses. Under the Tudors, "the prophecies were no longer frustrating promises of future greatness and native sovereignty but had now achieved fulfillment in the Tudor victory."[143] Henry would employ the symbols of Arthurian legend to his political advantage throughout his reign, even taking great care to ensure that his first-born son, Arthur, was born at Winchester – the site of the fabled Camelot -- so that he might fulfill the prophecy.[144] Long after Henry VII, the Tudors right through to Elizabeth I would continue to appropriate these legends to bolster the royal image.[145]

Denys Hay has acknowledged in his study of Polydore Vergil's work that the humanist's "historical integrity is most severely tested" when his history reaches the events of the fifteenth century and the rise of the Tudor house.[146] Vergil was commissioned to write a history that favoured and defended Henry VII's dynasty to the courts of Europe; he did this so well that, as Hay puts it, "its results are still with us."[147] Vergil achieved this partly through the reporting of prophecies; precisely the kind of causative explanation that he had rejected for earlier periods. In his discussion of the first year of Henry VII's reign, he makes a peculiar reference to the Merlinic prophecy of Cadwallader – the very same with which the people of Worcester greeted Henry. In Geoffrey of Monmouth's *Historia Regum Britannie,* Cadwallader, the last king of the Britons, who was determined to regain his dominions from the Anglo-Saxons, heard the voice of an angel telling him to "desist from his enterprise."[148] The angel told Cadwallader that God did not wish for the Britons to rule any longer and that he was to go to Pope Sergius and do penance. Only Cadwallader's sacrifice of power would bring about a future victory of the Britons over the

---

[142] John Leland, *De Rebus Britannicis Collectanea,* ed. Thomas Hearne, (London (1770), 196; Sydney Anglo, "The British History in Early Tudor Propaganda," *Bulletin of the John Rylands Library* 44 (1962), 1; Dobin, *Merlin's Disciples,* 51.

[143] Hughes, *Arthurian Myths and Alchemy,* 117-118; Dobin, *Merlin's Disciples,* 51.

[144] Hughes, *Arthurian Myths and Alchemy,* 307.

[145] Dobin, *Merlin's Disciples.*

[146] Hay, *Polydore Vergil,* 154.

[147] Ibid.

[148] Geoffrey of Monmouth, *History of the Kings of Britain,* trans. Aaron Thompson, (Cambridge, Ontario: In Parentheses Publications, 1999), 212.

Anglo-Saxons. The Britons, through "the merit of their faith, should again recover the island, when the time decreed for it was come."[149] It was this same prophecy, taken from Geoffrey of Monmouth's manuscript, that Vergil used to create a sense of inevitability around Henry's victory at Bosworth and make it appear that he was always destined to rule. After describing Henry VII's victory over Richard III and his entrance into London like "a triumphing general," Vergil describes the coronation as "an event of which foreknowledge had been possible both many centuries earlier and also soon after his birth." Borrowing heavily from the *Historia Regum Britannie,* the text relates how "797 years before, there came one night to Cadwallader, some sort of apparition with a heavenly appearance," and this appearance foretold, "how long afterwards it would come to pass that his descendents would recover the land."[150] According to Vergil's interpretation, this prophecy came true in Henry VII who was actively projecting himself as the heir to the great kings of Britain.[151]

That Vergil was under Tudor patronage explains why the Italian scholar would borrow and appropriate a Merlinic prophecy to bolster the claim of Henry VII from Geoffrey of Monmouth, a source that, earlier in his own work, he had fervently discredited. Having been "courteously received by the king and ever after [...] entertained by him kindly,"[152] Vergil enjoyed a relationship of patronage with the first Tudor king, one that was continued under Henry VIII. Although Vergil may have begun his labour with the intent to do away with inaccuracies in writing the *Historia,* it is clear that the wishes of his patron, Henry VII, took precedence and Vergil did not wish to risk losing such a valuable relationship. As in previous reigns, the patronage system under the first two Tudors extended through the whole of English society. With the king as the ultimate patron, maintaining loyalty through the awarding of titles, property, church livings and gifts from the royal coffers, this system trickled downward into every level of society.[153] English social hierarchy was, as Alistair Fox argues, "maintained by it, and the whole government of England depended upon its smooth operation."[154] The patronage system was vital for those who made their careers as artists and writers. The royal family and the nobility often employed those who were learned in the liberal arts to be tutors to their children. Men of letters

---

[149] Geoffrey of Monmouth, *History of the Kings of Britain,* 212.

[150] Vergil, *The Anglica Historia of Polydore Vergil,* 4-5.

[151] Vergil, *The Anglica Historia of Polydore Vergil,* 5.

[152] Hay, *Polydore Vergil,* 4.

[153] Fox, *Politics and Literature,* 11.

[154] Ibid.

under the patronage of the king and England's noble families could also be employed as legal officers, ambassadors to the crown or as chaplains and secretaries.[155] Alistair Fox's study of the literary patronage system displays how essential it was for scholars to find patrons to support them directly or to find someone who was in a position to influence potential patrons. Of course there were mutual benefits to these kinds of relationships as not only did the men of letters need the support of wealthy patrons to continue their works, the patron also benefitted from investing their support. For example, after winning the English throne and spending years staving off pretenders who incited rebellion within the realm, Henry VII needed to consolidate and bolster his power as the head of a new dynasty. As part of a "major campaign to amplify the magnificence of his rule" the new king commissioned tapestries, pageants and, as we have seen, he employed several artists and men of letters.[156] These men were tasked with writing the Tudors into British history through encomia that would project Henry as the "prophesied and true heir of the ancient British kings."[157] Polydore Vergil was one of those employed to write a narrative that amplified the magnificence and power of the Tudors, even if doing so conflicted with his original aspirations for the work. The demands of patronage required him to make use of Geoffrey of Monmouth's text to create an image of the king that was both consistent with what the crown was projecting and would ensure that the patron-artist relationship remained intact. This accounts for the peculiar inconsistencies between the first several books of the *Historia,* and the book covering Henry VII's reign.

As a man of letters who owed his status and wealth in England to the patronage of Henry VII, Vergil did not stop short of using the Arthurian legends and Merlinic prophesies and employed a variety of other devices to achieve the desired story arcs and tropes. Consequently, the twenty-sixth and twenty-seventh books of the *Historia* covering the reigns of Henry VII and Henry VIII are laden with references to *fortuna* and divine providence which were used in a similar way to the Arthurian legends. These created both a sense of inevitability and destiny around the rise of the Tudors, that God himself had chosen them to rule. For instance, Henry VII's marriage to Elizabeth of York in 1485 was hailed by Vergil as the product of divine intervention:

---

[155] Fox, *Politics and Literature*, 11.
[156] Fox, *Politics and Literature*, 17.
[157] Ibid.

> He then took in marriage Elizabeth, daughter of Edward, a
> woman indeed intelligent above all others, and equally
> beautiful. It is legitimate to attribute this to divine
> intervention, for plainly by it all things which nourished the
> two most ruinous factions were utterly removed, by it the two
> houses of Lancaster and York were united and from the union
> the true and established royal line emerged which now
> reigns.[158]

In writing of the union in this manner, Vergil was once again enveloping the Tudor dynasty with a sense of providence and giving credence to the image of Henry VII as the king who ended the Wars of the Roses. No longer was the realm and its nobility torn in half by crippling civil war and this was all because of Henry's victory at Bosworth and his subsequent marriage to Elizabeth. With Henry's tenuous claim to the throne, the marriage came to hold strategic and political significance and steps were taken very shortly after the Tudor victory at Bosworth to ensure that it took place. On 16 January 1486, at the special request of the king and the queen and through the intercession of Archbishop John Morton, Pope Innocent issued a papal dispensation for the marriage, which was confirmed on 27 March.[159] What is especially significant about the dispensation was that it "pronounced *ipso facto* excommunication against anyone challenging the marriage or Henry's right to the throne."[160] The dispensation also stressed that Henry's right did not depend on his marriage to Elizabeth.[161] As the court appointed historian, Polydore Vergil adopted a stance that corroborated this and painted the union as the will of God.

That Vergil would make use of *fortuna* and providence is not surprising given the importance of these themes within humanist scholarship. Ideas about *fortuna* and providence were woven into traditions of history writing since antiquity and the humanists' emulation of classical authors meant that they frequently made use of these concepts. From antiquity through the middle ages and into the age of humanism, scholars were debating the philosophical problems about human destiny and human action. For instance, Dante Alighieri's fourteenth century *Divina*

---

[158] Vergil, *The Anglica Historia of Polydore Vergil*, 7.

[159] Davies, "Bishop John Morton, the Holy See and the Accession of Henry VII," 14; Pope Innocent VIII, "The dispensation for the marriage of Henry VII and Elizabeth of York," in *The Reign of Henry VII from Contemporary Sources vol. 1,* ed. A.F. Pollard, (New York: Bombay:Calcutta: Longmans, Greens and Co., 1913).

[160] Davies, "Bishop John Morton", 15; Pope Innocent VIII, "The dispensation for the marriage of Henry VII and Elizabeth of York".

[161] Ibid.

Commedia does not hold the malice of men as the product of providence or *fortuna*. God bestowed upon man the intelligence and the ability "to perceive the good and to follow it in his actions." Although man's inclination to evil is subject to the whims of providence and *fortuna,* virtue is powerful enough to conquer it.[162] Also the fourteenth century, Petrarch's *De remediis utriusque fortunae* reached a very similar conclusion. Building on the work of Boethius, he explored how "human virtue and reason can withstand fortune's relentless claims."[163] This view would influence humanist scholars from Boccaccio's *Decameron* well into the Renaissance.[164] What is interesting is that Vergil seems to diverge from the traditional humanist view that the virtue of man could overcome fortune or providence. It appears that Vergil once again put the wishes of his patron to the fore through his unorthodox manipulation of literary devices. In this way, he could employ them to achieve narrative tropes that would corroborate Tudor propaganda efforts. Denys Hay writes that "to read the *Anglica Historia* is to obtain an impression of an England where the central thread of continuity lies in the succession of kings, where change is the product of royal action, where immutable human nature and mutable fortune play a never-ending game punctuated by rare interventions of divine justice."[165] For the most part, Vergil observes this in the *Historia*, however it is an entirely different matter when he broaches the subject of Henry VII's reign, particularly the king's reputation towards the end of his life.

In Vergil's chapter on the year 1502, he writes that after having subdued the conspiracy of Edmund de la Pole to challenge him for the throne, Henry VII could at last "relax his mind in peace." But alas the king became preoccupied with a new worry, "for he began to treat his people with more harshness and severity than had been his custom, in order (as he himself asserted) to ensure they remained more thoroughly and entirely in obedience to him."[166] Vergil acknowledges at this point that the people believed that they were not suffering "on account of their own sins, but on account of the greed of their monarch."[167] He also acknowledges that although "nothing could be found wanting in King Henry," he gradually sank into avarice. Vergil attributed this change in Henry VII's demeanor as the product of *fortuna*:

---

[162] Antonino Poppi, "Problems of Knowledge and Action: Fate, Fortune, Providence and Human Freedom," in *The Cambridge History of Renaissance Philosophy,* ed. Charles B. Schmitt, Quentin Skinner, Eckhard Kessler and Jill Kraye (Cambridge: Cambridge University Press, 1988), 641 – 667.
[163] Poppi, "Problems of Knowledge and Action," 645.
[164] Ibid.
[165] Hay, *Polydore Vergil*, 136.
[166] Vergil, *The Anglica Historia of Polydore Vergil*, 127.
[167] Ibid.

> Evil fortune blighted Henry in this manner so that he, who
> already excelled other princes in his many virtues, should not
> also be pre-eminent in subduing all vices.[168]

Avarice, he wrote, "now [...] dominated and penetrated into all activities" and it brought misery to the people of the realm without truly satiating the concerns of Henry VII, who was said to be aware that his subjects feared him rather than loved him.[169] Here Vergil was echoing the words of Milanese envoy Giovanni de Bebulcho, who wrote to the Secretary of the Duke of Milan in 1496. De Bebulcho was reporting on a conversation with a Florentine who was visiting London. In their conversation, the Florentine told de Bebulcho that "[Henry VII] is rather feared than loved, and this was due to his avarice."[170] The Florentine also claimed "the king is very powerful in money, but if fortune allowed some lord of the blood royal to rise and he had to take the field, he would fare badly owing to his avarice; his people would abandon him."[171] De Bebulcho's correspondence provides insight on the extent to which Henry VII's reputation for avarice and public sentiment against him actually transcended the borders of England to reach diplomats from the Italian city states.

Despite the king's very public reputation for greed and cruelty, the subject of Henry VII's avarice in the later years of his reign was nonetheless a delicate one around which Vergil had to navigate. After his death in 1509, Henry VII stood accused of avarice by his former subjects, prompting Henry VIII to distance himself from his father's policies so that he might avoid similar charges.[172] Yet it would still be impolitic for the official historian to criticize too openly. Ergo, Vergil, who retained royal patronage upon the accession of the new king, found himself steering these tumultuous waters as best he could. Thus, various passages in the *Historia* excuse the avarice and greed of the first Tudor king as a combination of a series of accidents and bad fortune. His most trusted counselors, John Morton, Archbishop of Canterbury, and Reginald Bray died within three years of one another; Morton died in 1500 followed by Bray in 1503. Vergil writes that after their deaths it was "obvious to all these that these two were above all responsible

---

[168] Vergil, *The Anglica Historia of Polydore Vergil*, 127.

[169] Vergil, *The Anglica Historia of Polydore Vergil*, 131.

[170] "Milan: 1496," in *Calendar of State Papers and Manuscripts in the Archives and Collections of Milan 1385-1618*, ed. Allen B Hinds (London: His Majesty's Stationery Office, 1912), 293-310, accessed March 12, 2016, http://www.british-history.ac.uk/cal-state-papers/milan/1385-1618/pp293-310.

[171] Ibid.

[172] Sydney Anglo, "Ill of the dead. The posthumous reputation of Henry VII," *Renaissance Studies* 1, no. 1 (1987), 29-30.

not for aggravating royal harshness against the people, but for restraining it."[173] Henry's greatest misfortune was the loss of his first-born son and heir, Arthur, to the English sweating sickness in April 1502. Less than a year later, in February 1503, Elizabeth of York died giving birth to a daughter who survived but a few days.[174] Henry's daughter Mary, who was betrothed to king James IV of Scotland, was also whisked away to be married, taking her place beside her husband.[175] Vergil's interpretation was that a combination of all these events served to harden the king and erode his just and virtuous character. No matter how virtuous he was, Henry was no match for the whims of lady fortune.

Despite his efforts to justify some of the king's actions after 1502, Vergil's sympathies towards Henry VII appear to have shifted significantly in the final portion of his chapter on the reign. While some of his commentary excused the king's behaviour as the result of bad fortune, Vergil appears to have become disillusioned with the actions of the king and at times he stopped just short of calling him a tyrant. One sees evidence of this in the way Vergil treated the subject of Henry VII's unpopularity and his fiscal policies enforced by Richard Empson and Edmund Dudley.[176] Henry's counselors were seen by many as instrumental in the implementation and execution of his unpopular policies, but even Vergil acknowledged that the blame also resided with the king. In one passage, which appears in both the manuscript and in the edition of 1534, Vergil places much of the blame for the actual extortion on Henry's counselors; yet we also see some of Vergil's criticisms of the regime slipping through as well:

> [Empson and Dudley] very soon claimed great weight with the monarch, and since they were educated men, he rapidly appointed them as judges to pronounce judicial sentence on wrongdoers. The pair, probably realizing they had been given the job by the king not so much to administer justice as to strip the population of its wealth, without respite and by every means fair or foul vied with each other in extorting money."[177]

---

[173] Vergil, *The Anglica Historia of Polydore Vergil*, 133-135.
[174] Vergil, *The Anglica Historia of Polydore Vergil*, 133.
[175] Vergil, *The Anglica Historia of Polydore Vergil*, 121, 135.
[176] Vergil, *The Anglica Historia of Polydore Vergil*, 129.
[177] Ibid.

The 1555 edition of the *Historia* also included a speech allegedly made by Edmund Dudley at his trial in 1509.[178] This speech was a last ditch effort by the former counselor to save his life by shifting the blame away from himself and Empson. Here he claimed that they had only been doing the king's bidding by enforcing the laws.[179] That Vergil included the speech of Edmund Dudley in his book on the reign of Henry VIII (published shortly following his death, after Vergil had returned to Italy for good) is perhaps indicative of his true thoughts on the late king, which he appears to have wrestled with in the face of his duty to his patrons. This struggle is evident in the final pages of the manuscript of Vergil's book on Henry VII. Here he provided a flattering physical description of the monarch, characterizing him as "gracious and kind" to the visitors of his court.[180] Vergil even acknowledged that Henry had many virtues and may have wanted to make amends for the way he had treated his subjects, but death took him before he had the chance.[181] Despite this, Vergil's closing statement on Henry VII in the manuscript of the *Historia* is strong and condemnatory:

> But all these virtues were obscured latterly only by avarice,
> from which (as we have showed above) he suffered. This
> avarice is surely a bad enough vice in a private individual,
> whom it forever torments; in a monarch indeed it may be
> considered the worst vice, since it is harmful to everyone, and
> distorts those qualities of trustfulness, justice and integrity by
> which the state must be governed.[182]

It is significant that Vergil actually used the term "avarice" to describe the king's actions after 1502. In his article, "Ill of the Dead. The posthumous reputation of Henry VII," Sydney Anglo stressed the difference between avarice and rapacity. He first argued that avarice and rapacity had much in common, but the thing that substantially differentiated one from the other was that avarice was one of the seven deadly sins.[183] "Avarice was especially vicious in a ruler for it was the mark of a tyrant – just as liberty was the mark of a virtuous prince"; therefore to accuse a ruler of avarice was essentially to accuse him of tyranny.[184] One might wonder how it is that Vergil could get away with saying such brazen things about Henry VII, especially since

---

[178] Vergil, *The Anglica Historia of Polydore Vergil*, 150.

[179] Vergil, *The Anglica Historia of Polydore Vergil*, 150-1.

[180] Vergil, *The Anglica Historia of Polydore Vergil*, 146.

[181] Ibid.

[182] Vergil, *The Anglica Historia of Polydore Vergil*, 147.

[183] Anglo, "Ill of the dead", 29-30.

[184] Ibid.

Henry VIII was to see a copy of the manuscript in circulation. But by the time of his death, as Sidney Anglo has argued, "Henry [VII] was thoroughly detested" by most of his subjects due to his stringent laws and the voracious efforts of the crown to fill the royal coffers.[185] Perhaps the accession of Henry VIII, who was not fond of his father, emboldened Vergil's sense of criticism (as it had with other scholars, such as Thomas More), especially as the new king, in a clever bout of public relations management, was actively making efforts to distance himself from the previous regime.[186] As long as Vergil, and other scholars, cloaked their criticisms and did not outright accuse Henry VII of tyranny, they were safe.

Fascinatingly, by the mid-1530s, with the printing of his *Historia* on the horizon, it seems Vergil would once again revert to curbing his criticisms of the regime. Prior to publication, he revised many of the passages about Henry VII that had appeared in the original manuscript. In many cases, Vergil removed them from the work altogether so that they did not appear in the 1534 edition. For instance, his final comments on Henry VII quoted above were among the many passages that were purged for the 1534 edition. Other deletions were more subtle but would certainly have raised questions had they been included in the widely circulated printed versions of the *Historia*. For example, although they appear in the manuscript, the names of Richard III's accomplices in the 1483 murder of Lord Hastings were removed from the *Historia* by 1534.[187] Hastings, a trusted agent of Edward IV, was killed by Richard III and several accomplices.[188] One of the accomplices named in the manuscript was Thomas Howard, Earl of Surrey, who was also alleged in the original manuscript to have helped in the murder of Richard III's nephews.[189] The Howards came to Richard III's defense when Henry Tudor challenged him for the throne, leading to Surrey's attainder in Henry VII's first parliament, where he was stripped of titles and lands before being thrown into the Tower of London. Thomas Howard was, however, able to get back into Henry VII's good graces, being reinstated as Earl of Surrey in 1487, and serving as

---

[185] Anglo, "Ill of the dead", 32.

[186] Ibid.

[187] Hay, *Polydore Vergil*, 204-205.

[188] Rosemary Horrox, "Hastings, William, first Baron Hastings (*c.*1430–1483)", *Oxford Dictionary of National Biography*, Oxford University Press, 2004 [http://0-www.oxforddnb.com.mercury.concordia.ca/view/article/12588, accessed 10 Jan 2016]; Hay, *Polydore Vergil*, 204-205.

[189] Hay, *Polydore Vergil*, 204-205.

executor of the king's will in 1509.[190] Surrey also played a prominent role in Henry VII's funeral procession as well as in the coronation of Henry VIII.[191] Additionally, while the king "played at war with France," in1513 the earl of Surrey stopped an invasion from Scotland in what is known as the battle of Flodden, earning "one of the kingdom's greatest victories."[192] Surrey was rewarded for his faithful service to the crown on 1 February 1514 when he was created duke of Norfolk and his son, Thomas, was named earl of Surrey. Under the Tudors, the Howards would arguably become the most influential and powerful magnates in the realm.[193] Vergil must have realized the embarrassment that could come from immortalizing into English history the implication of such a prominent agent of the crown in the deaths of Lord Hastings and the heirs of Edward IV. Instead, all printed edition of the *Historia* from 1534 onward simply refer to Richard III's accomplices in the murder as "other lords,"[194] which was a far safer alternative.

In a similar vein, Vergil's 1534 account of Thomas Grey's desertion of Henry Tudor's cause on the eve of the 1485 invasion from France is remarkably less detailed than his rendition of the same event in the manuscript.[195] Thomas Grey, first Marquess of Dorset, who was Elizabeth Woodville's son from her first marriage and the half brother of Elizabeth of York, was attainted for treason by Richard III in 1484 and fled to France to join Henry Tudor's followers as they planned an invasion of England. It appears, however, that Dorset had a change of heart when he heard that his mother had made peace with Richard III in August 1485 shortly before the invasion, and he attempted to desert the Tudor cause by fleeing to England. Dorset was instead intercepted by Lancastrian forces and detained in France until Henry became king. Henry magnanimously reversed Dorset's treason attainder and allowed him to return to England.[196] For the 1534 edition of the *Historia*, Vergil opted for a version that was far more convenient. According to the revised version, Dorset was "cauled home of his mother" and after fleeing he

---

[190] David M. Head, "Howard, Thomas, second duke of Norfolk (1443–1524)", *Oxford Dictionary of National Biography*, Oxford University Press, 2004; online edn, Sept 2012 [http://0-www.oxforddnb.com.mercury.concordia.ca/view/article/13939, accessed 6 March 2016].

[191] Head, "Howard, Thomas, second duke of Norfolk (1443–1524)"; Chrimes, *Henry VII*, 27-28.

[192] Head, "Howard, Thomas, second duke of Norfolk (1443–1524)".

[193] Ibid.

[194] Vergil, *Three Books of Polydore Vergil's English,* 180.

[195] Hay, *Polydore Vergil*, 205-206.

[196] T. B. Pugh, "Grey, Thomas, first marquess of Dorset (*c.*1455–1501)", *Oxford Dictionary of National Biography*, Oxford University Press, 2004 [http://0-www.oxforddnb.com.mercury.concordia.ca/view/article/11560, accessed 10 Jan 2016].

was persuaded to come back by Humphrey Cheney.[197] This way, Vergil wasn't running the risk of insulting the next generation of Greys, who were still prominent agents of the crown under Henry VIII (his great granddaughter, Lady Jane Grey, would be queen for thirteen days after the death of Edward VI in 1553).[198] Nor was Vergil drawing attention to the fact that the half-brother of Henry VII's bride-to-be had actually lost faith and deserted the Tudor cause – a cause that was portrayed as divinely ordained by both Tudor propaganda efforts and Vergil's own work.

Perhaps the most interesting deletion of all was Vergil's censoring of Henry Tudor's reaction to the news in early 1485 that Richard III intended to marry Henry's own intended bride, Elizabeth of York.[199] According to Vergil's manuscript, when news reached Henry that Richard intended to marry Elizabeth, Henry instead offered his hand to a sister of Sir Walter Herbert of Raglan, the head of a prominent Welsh family, in an attempt to bolster his support in Wales. Vergil further asserted that since his youth, Henry, who grew up as a ward of the Herbert household, had loved Sir Walter's eldest sister, Maud.[200] Historians have given some credence to this story: Henry stood the best chance at success if he could earn the loyalty of some of the great Welsh families and this was something he could easily achieve through a calculated marriage alliance.[201] By 1485, Maud was already married to Henry Percy, earl of Northumberland, therefore Henry set his sights on the younger Herbert sisters.[202] Not only would such a marriage provide him with the Welsh alliance he coveted, it would also help him cultivate a relationship with Henry Percy, a powerful magnate in the north, through the bonds of extended family. Of course, the plans were scrapped and Henry married Elizabeth instead. But just as Henry VII's reign was projected as a product of divine providence, his marriage to Elizabeth of York was similarly portrayed. The story of his courtship of the Herbert sisters would have undermined such a view and thus Vergil must have believed it was best to remove it altogether. As a result, the editions of the *Historia* after 1534 only make a passing reference to Richard III's plans to marry Elizabeth, while the ordeal with the Herbert sisters is completely omitted.[203]

---

[197] Polydore Vergil, *Three Books of Polydore Vergil's English History*, 214.

[198] Pugh, "Grey, Thomas, first marquess of Dorset (*c.*1455–1501)".

[199] Hay, *Polydore Vergil*, 206.

[200] Ibid.

[201] Davies "Information, disinformation and political knowledge," 248, 251.

[202] Hay, *Polydore Vergil*, 206.

[203] Vergil, *Three Books of Polydore Vergil's English History*, 212-213.

Henry VIII's personal and political turmoil in the 1520s and 30s may have contributed to Vergil's sentiments that it was better to delete the politically sensitive statements about Henry VII – especially since there would be a markedly higher rate of circulation for a printed book than there had been for a single manuscript. Notably, the king's behaviour from the 1520s onward would be a stark contrast to the good natured, charismatic version of Henry that had succeeded the throne. As the years trickled by this was probably aggravated by the king's anxieties over his lack of issue, a situation historians have named "the king's great matter."[204] After nearly twenty years of marriage, Catherine of Aragon had failed to give him an heir, and by 1527 Henry began looking for a way out of the marriage, a move that J.J Scarisbrick has dubbed "dynastically urgent."[205] After 1530, the events leading to Henry's break with Rome occurred in rapid succession, culminating with the Act of Supremacy, which declared him the head of Church and State in 1534.[206]

In the thick of Henry's crisis with Rome and his concerns over producing an heir to his throne, 1534 was also the year that Polydore Vergil's *Anglica Historia* was first printed in Latin at Basel. Given the tumultuous state of affairs in the England of the 1530s, passages and criticism that embarrassed the dynasty would have hit much closer to home. As long as the criticism towards Henry VII was not overt, it seemed Vergil, and many others, could get away with it for a time. It was quite another story to taint or embarrass the Tudor line as this had direct bearing on Henry VIII, who perceived that legitimation was now more important than ever, and whose dynastic concerns contributed to his increasing volatility. The research of Denys Hay and C.S.L. Davies indicates that Vergil was fearful of the English political climate of the 1530s and this would have been an influence on his editing of the *Historia.* According to Hay, the near twenty-year delay between the manuscript and the 1534 edition "was probably due to the author's anxiety lest the political situation should make publication unadvisable." Vergil may have decided to print in 1534 because he believed that with Henry's marriage to Anne Boleyn, "the crisis which had begun in 1527 might well have seemed over for good."[207] Davies states in his article on information and disinformation under Henry VII and Henry VIII that while Vergil may have preferred the superior printing standards in Basel, "it may be that political sensitivities made

---

[204] Ives, "Henry VIII (1491–1547)"; Scarisbrick, *Henry VIII,* 150.
[205] Scarisbrick, *Henry VIII,* 152.
[206] Ives, "Henry VIII (1491–1547)".
[207] Hay, *Polydore Vergil,* 82.

him cautious about publishing in England."[208] As a result of the anxieties he harbored about the political situation in England at the time, we can then surmise that Vergil had begun a practice of self-censoring in order to make sure that he did not publish anything that would get him in trouble. This resulted in a version of the *Historia* that contained far less damning statements about Henry VII, and involved the removal or modification of anecdotes and passages that would have embarrassed the royal family or directly opposed the message being disseminated by Tudor propaganda efforts. It may also be significant that in 1534, Thomas More was arrested for treason on the grounds that he refused to swear his allegiance to the parliamentary Act of Succession that disinherited Catherine's and Henry's daughter, Mary.[209] Vergil may have believed that censorship was the best route if he did not wish to follow More into prison. This can be further corroborated by Vergil's omission of the book on the reign of Henry VIII from the 1534 and 1546 editions respectively, which he may have felt would not please the king as it contained details of the divorce proceedings with Catherine, as well as many unpleasantries about Cardinal Wolsey.[210]

Details of Henry VIII's reign appeared only in the 1555 edition of the *Historia*, after the death of the king and as Vergil himself was dying. This was long after Vergil had returned permanently to Italy on the request of Edward VI, who wished for the Italian scholar to "visit and see, nowe in his old age, his said natyve country and there to make his abode during his pleasure."[211] As a reward for his faithful service to Henry VII, Henry VIII and Edward VI, Vergil was allowed to live out the rest of his days in Italy while enjoying the rents and profits of the office he held in England without fear that these would be forfeited.[212] By the time his final edition of the *Historia* was printed, Vergil was far away and no longer had to fear retribution from the crown. He died shortly after on 18 April 1555 and "it was fitting that in the year of his death the *Anglica Historia* should at last include the final book narrating the events of Henry VIII's reign."[213] Unsurprisingly, we shall see that the fear and uncertainty that plagued the Italian scholar during his time in England inspired similar attempts at self-censorship and concealment in the works of his friend, Thomas More.

---

[208] Davies "Information, disinformation and political knowledge", 241.

[209] Marius, *Thomas More*, 461.

[210] Hay, *Polydore Vergil*, 83.

[211] Davies "Information, disinformation and political knowledge", 241; Hay, *Polydore Vergil*, 20.

[212] Polydore Vergil, *Three Books of Polydore Vergil's English History*, 303; Hay, *Polydore Vergil*, 20.

[213] Hay, *Polydore Vergil*, 21.

Chapter 4: Thomas More's *History of King Richard III* and *Utopia*

Thomas More (1478-1535) was an English humanist scholar and lawyer from a wealthy London family involved in both trade and the law. His father, John More, rose to become serjeant-at-law in 1503, justice of the common pleas in 1518 and justice of King's Bench in 1520.[214] He also had a close connection with Archbishop John Morton, one of Henry VII's closest counselors. John More's connections paved the way for Thomas More to study Latin at London's finest grammar school, St. Anthony's, in which he received training in early Ciceronian rhetoric that would prepare him for a career as a lawyer and, eventually, his service to the crown. As a boy, More served in Archbishop Morton's household, and then with Morton's patronage proceeded to Canterbury College, Oxford in 1492.[215] Between 1494 and 1510, by which time he was in his early thirties, More would complete his time at Oxford and settle into the life of a London lawyer, while establishing connections with the intellectual circle of John Colet, Thomas Linacre, William Grocyn, and William Lily, as well as a lifelong friendship with Desiderius Erasmus.[216]

The first significant modern study of the English humanist was R.W. Chambers' *Thomas More*, published in 1935. Chambers sought to challenge a traditional view held by scholars that Thomas More, the humanist author of *Utopia,* was in conflict with the Thomas More who was seen as a martyr after being executed by Henry VIII in 1535. It can be argued that Chambers' work did for More what Hay achieved for Vergil, as the London native's personal life appears to receive a fuller treatment than in earlier biographies. Thomas Betteridge's 2013 study, *Writing Faith and Telling Tales* argues that although "Chambers insisted in his work that More's life and work exhibit a basic coherence," he paints a rather simplistic view of the Middle Ages as a time without major conflict or areas of dispute. What seems to frustrate Betteridge in particular is the way that Chambers "depicted More's religion [Catholicism] as entirely conventional without pausing to consider what this meant for Medieval England."[217] It appears that Betteridge was not the only critic of Chambers' work, as in 1985 Richard Marius published his own biography of

---

[214] Marius, "The Beginnings," in *Thomas More,* 3-13; Seymour Baker House, "More, Sir Thomas (1478–1535)," *Oxford Dictionary of National Biography*, Oxford University Press, 2004; online edn, Jan 2008 [http://0-www.oxforddnb.com.mercury.concordia.ca/view/article/19191, accessed 10 Jan 2016].

[215] Ibid.

[216] Ibid.

[217] Betteridge, *Writing Faith and Telling Tales,* 4.

Thomas More. Marius's More appears to be a man who, throughout his life, could not forgive himself for giving into his sexual desires and marrying his first wife, Jane Colt. Marius argues that More became bitter, watching "while his world seemed to be going speedily to hell" under the weight of the English Reformation. In his article "Sir Thomas More and the Opposition to Henry VIII," G.R. Elton appears to share Marius' sense that More, in the 1530s, was a man caught between competing demands. However, Elton sees these demands as an excessive hatred of heresy and recognition of the need for reform.[218] Betteridge feels that Elton's discussion of More was critical and strangely uncomprehending, writing that "It is clear that he found it simply impossible to understand More, or forgive him for being, a man of reason, a humanist, the writer of *Utopia*, and a principled opponent of the policies pursued by the Henrician regime in pursuits of Henry's divorce of Catherine of Aragon."[219]

Before becoming an opponent of the crown's policies in the 1530s, More spent the years between 1504 and 1517 cultivating relationships with other scholars and establishing his career as a lawyer and civil servant in London. His activities during this time reveal that he did have aspirations for royal patronage. Alistair Fox's study on literary patronage under the Tudors ventures that for reasons of ideological conflict with older scholars under the patronage of Henry VII, the younger humanists such as Erasmus, More and Linacre were out of favour with the crown until the accession of Henry VIII.[220] Bernard André, one of Henry VII's historians and tutor to prince Arthur, allegedly tried to prevent Thomas Linacre from succeeding him in his position as royal tutor by turning the king against Linacre.[221] More's son-in-law, William Roper, wrote a biography of More in the 1550s titled *The Life of Sir Thomas More*, which was eventually published by the Jesuits in 1626.[222] This biography was meant to accompany a list of More's unpublished works and it served as part of a family campaign to justify More's resistance to the policies of Henry VIII in the 1530s. According to Roper's biography, More may have muddled an opportunity to enter into royal service when he allegedly opposed the king in parliament in 1504 over a request for money for the marriage of the king's daughter Mary to

---

[218] G.R. Elton, "Sir Thomas More and the Oppression to Henry VIII," in *Essential Articles for the Study of Thomas More*, ed. R.S. Sylvester and G.P. Marc'hadour (Hamden: Archon Books, 1977), 79-91.

[219] Betteridge, *Writing Faith and Telling Tales*, 6.

[220] Fox, *Politics and Literature*, 15-17.

[221] Ibid.

[222] Hugh Trevor-Roper, "Roper, William (1495x8–1578)", *Oxford Dictionary of National Biography*, Oxford University Press, 2004; online edn, May 2005 [http://0-www.oxforddnb.com.mercury.concordia.ca/view/article/24074, accessed 6 March 2016].

James IV of Scotland. Roper claimed that in order to exact revenge on More for his opposition in Parliament, Henry had his father, John More, imprisoned in the Tower of London and would only release him for a sum of £100.[223] According to the parliament rolls of 1504, Thomas More was indeed present at the session and was one of those who opposed the king in his request.[224] However, Roper's allegation that Henry VII imprisoned John More in the Tower as an act of revenge cannot be corroborated and is likely a fabrication.[225] To be sure, whether Roper's tale carries any weight, More's role in the defeat of Henry's request for money in Parliament would not earn him favour from the crown, and like many other progressive humanist scholars he would have to wait until Henry VIII's coronation in 1509.

When Henry VIII took the throne, there was a "cultural purge as well as a political one among the king's servants."[226] Not only were Richard Empson and Edmund Dudley arrested and executed, many scholars and artists who had enjoyed the patronage of Henry VII were dismissed by the new monarch and their positions filled by others, most likely in the new king's attempt to present a new and improved regime to the realm.[227] Notably, Henry VIII was "less consciously concerned to amplify the magnificence of his court through literature"[228] than Henry VII had been; instead the new king preferred elaborate jousting tournaments, displays of pageantry and entertainments.[229] More would not enter into royal service until 1518. He did however, write a series of flattering Latin poems in 1509 as a gift to Henry VIII, most likely in a quest for royal patronage. In the meantime, More worked as the undersheriff of London and undertook trade and diplomatic missions, including a visit to Antwerp in 1515 during which he purportedly met with the fictional Raphael Hythloday as well as his real-life friend, Peter Giles.[230]

Although the vast historiography of Thomas More has inspired an array of debates, scholars of his life and works agree that More had an particular aversion to tyranny. Erasmus

---

[223] William Roper, *The Life of Sir Thomas More,* ed. Sir Joseph Walton (London: Burns & Oates, 1905), 7-8.

[224] "Henry VII: January 1504," in *Parliament Rolls of Medieval England,* ed. Chris Given-Wilson, Paul Brand, Seymour Phillips, Mark Ormrod, Geoffrey Martin, Anne Curry and Rosemary Horrox (Woodbridge: Boydell, 2005), accessed January 15, 2016, http://www.british-history.ac.uk/no-series/parliament-rolls-medieval/january-1504.

[225] Marius, *Thomas More,* xv-xvi.

[226] Fox, *Politics and Literature,* 19.

[227] Ibid.

[228] Fox, *Politics and Literature,* 19.

[229] Sharpe, *Selling the Tudor Monarchy,* 157-160.

[230] House, "More, Sir Thomas (1478–1535)".

wrote in a letter to Ulrich von Hutten on 23 July 1519 that More always had a "special hatred of absolute rule and a corresponding love for equality."[231] More's hatred for despotism is apparent in his 1509 coronation ode to Henry VIII. In this gift to the eighteen-year-old Henry, More praises him as a king "who is worthy not merely to govern a single people but singly to rule the whole world,"[232] while making his distaste for the policies of Henry VII well known. Henry VIII had liberated the people of England from "fear, harm, danger and grief," and he brought peace, joy and laughter back to the realm.[233] In several passages, More makes a multitude of references to the infamous fiscal policies enforced under the previous regime and the corruption of the legal system under Richard Empson and Edmund Dudley, all of which inspired "distressing fear" among English subjects. With the accession of the new king the laws could at last regain "their proper authority."[234] The people no longer had to hide their possessions for fear that they would be taken away, and no longer was it a crime for them to own property that was honestly acquired (More makes the sarcastic remark that previously this was a very serious offence). In case it was not plain enough whom he was criticizing, More even made direct reference to Henry VII in mentioning how the new king, "decided to retract certain provisions of the law which he knew his father had approved."[235] Now that England had a new king, its people were liberated and tyranny might at last be vanquished.

Having borne witness to the rapacity of Henry VII, More was deeply skeptical about the institution of kingship.[236] Although he did not hold back in his scathing remarks about the previous regime, the coronation ode was not only written as a critique of the fiscal and legal policies of Henry VII, nor merely as an opportunity to praise the new king. His admiration made plain, More took the opportunity to caution the young Henry that "unlimited power has a tendency to weaken good minds, and that even in the case of very gifted men."[237] Thus, he was counseling Henry to be careful not to let power corrupt him, lest he become the same kind of ruler as his father. Evidently this was something that worried More and he hoped that Henry would continue to be the kind of ruler who had a "sense of responsibility in the treatment of his

---

[231] Desiderius Erasmus, "Letter 999," in *The Correspondence of Erasmus, Vol. 7*, trans. R.A.B. Mynors, D.F.S. Thomson, (Toronto: University of Toronto Press, 1982), 18.
[232] More, "Epigram 19",101.
[233] More, "Epigram 19",105.
[234] More, "Epigram 19",103.
[235] More, "Epigram 19", 107.
[236] Fox, *Politics and Literature*, 113.
[237] More, "Epigram 19", 105.

people"[238] and put the good of the realm before monetary gain. It is generally agreed among Morean scholars that he wrote *The History of King Richard III* (1513) and *Utopia* (1515) as a way to come to terms with the tyranny of the past and to warn against the possibility that such a beast might rise again.[239] More's interest in history was neither casual nor dutiful. He had developed "anxieties about the institution of kingship and the possibility that it could become abused in his own time" and he looked to history for answers, developing an interest in the usurpation and deposition of Richard III.[240]

Thomas More's *History of Richard III* was composed sometime between 1513 and 1519 - John Rastell dated the work to "about the yeare of our Lorde. 1513."[241] For the purposes of this thesis, Richard S. Sylvester's English edition of *Richard III* will be used. More wrote two versions of the history, one in Latin and one in English, which Sylvester's edition delivers to us through a collation of five texts that each drew on More's manuscript. These texts include two 1543 editions of *The chronicle of Iohn Hardyng*, the 1548 and 1550 editions of Edward Hall's *The Union of the two noble and illustre families of Lancastre and Yorke* and John Rastell's English collection of More's works, published in 1557.[242] More left both versions of *Richard III* unfinished and the works were published posthumously, the most circulated version being John Rastell's English publication in 1557.[243]

The *History of Richard III* opens with an account of the final year of Edward IV's reign and his death in 1483. The late king left behind a widow and several children, including two sons, Edward and Richard, the oldest of which was *de jure* king. More's narrative traces the actions of Edward's brother, Richard, duke of Gloucester, who through devious and evil deeds elevated himself to the title of king of England in a matter of months, usurping the crown from his young nephew.[244] In More's work, Richard achieved this by securing a position as Lord Protector of the realm after convincing the members of the king's council of his devotion to the sons of Edward IV.[245] Richard was also guilty of the worst kind of evil by ordering the murder of Edward's two

---

[238] More, "Epigram 19", 105.

[239] Fox, *Politics and Literature*, 113; Betteridge, *Writing Faith and Telling Tales*, 42-43.

[240] Fox, *Politics and Literature*, 116.

[241] Betteridge, *Writing Faith and Telling Tales*, 40.

[242] More, "The History of King Richard III", xvii-xviii.

[243] Ibid.

[244] More, "The History of King Richard III".

[245] More, "The History of King Richard III", 24-25.

sons in the Tower of London to ensure that they would not be obstacles to him.[246] The titular character in More's narrative is, of course, Richard III, who is portrayed as evil incarnate, especially after he stoops to the level of nepoticide. More's Richard was a wretched man; even from infancy he "was malicious wrathful, enuious," and his own mother "had so muche a doe in her trauaile, that shee coulde not bee deliuered of hym uncutte."[247] His physical description as a little man with uneven shoulders and a hard face[248] places him in stark contrast with his strong, handsome and mighty older brother, Edward IV.[249] The unsightly appearance of the duke of Gloucester was representative of the evil inside him and such a description serves to reinforce Richard's character as a true villain and a tyrant, rejected by nature even from his very birth.

Although, as the title suggests, the work appears to be a history, literary scholars since the 1930s have argued that *Richard III* has a distinctly dramatic structure. A.F. Pollard's article on the making of *Richard III* lists several dramatic aspects of the work, which he believed characterized it as a drama with a historical subject[250] and in 1943 Leonard F. Dean wrote that the text had been "adequately studied as a historical document," but, as a drama, the work had not been given the same attention."[251] Similarly, Arthur Noel Kincaid, writing in 1972, expressed that "the dramatic aspect of [More's] writings has been all but ignored," and never carefully studied.[252] Even Richard S. Sylvester, whose authoritative edition of the text was published in 1963, acknowledged that *Richard III* is generally accepted as a history, but with a certain dramatic forcefulness.[253] Thomas Betteridge also acknowledges that More placed "Richard's succession within a dramatic framework," and that More's use of "image places" in the work places it "alongside a number of political plays produced during the 1510s."[254] The inclusion of *dramatis personae* in the opening pages is a staple of drama as are the inclusion of numerous speeches and the use of dialogue and More's avoidance of dates throughout the work.[255] That Thomas More was very interested in drama and was connected to theatre through various family

---

[246] More, "The History of King Richard III".
[247] More, "The History of King Richard III", 7.
[248] Ibid.
[249] More, "The History of King Richard III", 4.
[250] Pollard, "The Making of Sir Thomas More's Richard III," 230.
[251] Dean, "Literary Problems", 22.
[252] Kincaid, "The Dramatic Structure," 223.
[253] More, "The History of King Richard III", lxxx.
[254] Betteridge, *Writing Faith and Telling Tales,* 43.
[255] More, "The History of King Richard III", lxxx; Pollard, "The Making of Sir Thomas More's Richard III", 230.

relations reveals that the dramatic aspects of the work were not entirely out of place. More was related by marriage to dramatist John Heywood, and his brother-in-law John Rastell owned a stage at his estate.[256] William Roper's *Life of Sir Thomas More* also describes how a young More, in the service of John Morton, allegedly impressed the archbishop at Christmas-time theatre performances when he would suddenly "step in among the other players, and never studying for the matter take a part of his own there presently among them."[257] More's affinity for drama and theatre is confirmed in Erasmus' 1519 letter to Ulrich von Hutten. After a lengthy description of his friend's appearance and character, Erasmus recounts how the young More "wrote brief comedies and acted in them."[258] An interest in drama, cultivated from a young age, as well as a growing ambiguity about the institution of kingship and the rise of tyranny, culminated in the writing of *Richard III* in which More attempted to demonstrate "the nature of tyranny and its evil results."[259] While his subject was a historical one, More could script his characters' actions along the lines of a morality play, which was facilitated through the use of irony as well as the dramatic structure of the work. Thus, the end result is that the characters appear as actors on a stage, orating to the reader, who acts as the audience, about the evil of tyrants and the necessity of good government. As we have seen above, More's *Richard III* is difficult to classify as the work appears to borrow simultaneously from humanist techniques and themes as well as from the dramatic arts in its structure. Consquently, it is most helpful to consider *Richard III* as a historical representation, rather than a history in the modern sense.

Several analyses of Thomas More's *Richard III* have argued that More's juxtaposition of good and evil in the piece is reminiscent of moral exempla. R.W. Chambers has likened the work to a Greek tragedy, while A.R. Meyers has stated that *Richard III* is the "renaissance equivalent of a morality play."[260] This view is similar to that of Arthur Noel Kincaid, whose study on the dramaturgy of the piece concludes by calling it a "moral tragedy."[261] This not only connects More's work to the long medieval tradition of conveying moral lessons through drama, but also conforms to the humanist emphasis on the moral purposes of writing about the past.[262] If More

---

[256] Kincaid, "The Dramatic Structure", 226.
[257] Roper, *The Life of Sir Thomas More*, 4.
[258] Erasmus, "Letter 999", 19.
[259] Gransden, *Historical Writing in England vol.*, 445.
[260] A.R. Meyers, "The Character of Richard III," *History Today* 4 (1954), 515.
[261] Kincaid, "The Dramatic Structure", 242.
[262] Fox, *Politics and Literature*, 112.

were attempting to present *Richard III* as a kind of morality play on tyranny, while providing his readers with a cautionary tale that was based on real and relatively recent events, then it made sense to choose the reign of Richard III as his subject.[263] But then, this generates a perplexing set of observations about the portrayal of other characters in the work. If Richard III plays the part of More's tyrant, then in theory one would expect his other main character, Edward IV, to appear as the righteous king in the narrative, to create a juxtaposition of good versus evil. Even though Richard is portrayed as the epitome of evil, More's Edward IV is not wholly innocent either. In spite of the sympathy trumped up for Edward's character after Richard III seized his rightful heirs and allegedly had the young princes smothered in the Tower of London,[264] Edward was also a usurper who had deposed Henry VI, an anointed king.[265]

The obvious other candidate as "righteous king" for More's story of Richard III's fall – Henry Tudor – somewhat curiously does not appear in the narrative. The explanation for this may be as simple as that More did not finish the work, as it cuts off at Buckingham's rebellion in the fall of 1483,[266] well before one might expect Henry to appear (for instance, Henry does not appear in Shakespeare's play until Act V). Nonetheless, one suspects that it would have been difficult for More to resolve the dramatic and political problem that the portrayal of the young Henry Tudor – deposer of the tyrant Richard – would have posed for him. As he was writing *Richard III,* More was actively contemplating the difference between the actions of a good king and a bad one. His *Epigrammata,* a series of very short Latin poems written between 1500 and 1518, address kingship and tyranny as their main themes, and reveal that questions of governance and tyranny were very much on More's mind. Here he juxtaposes his definition of a good king and a bad king, almost as if he were writing a guide for the princes of the future, so that they might learn from the mistakes of the past. To More, a good king took on a paternalistic role, treating his subjects as his children and holding his power through the loyalty he inspired from them.[267] On the other hand, a bad king treated his subjects like slaves, and did not respect the laws of the realm.[268] A good king, like a sheep dog, was supposed to protect his flock from the

---

[263] Fox, *Politics and Literature*, 119.
[264] More, "The History of King Richard III", 85.
[265] More, "The History of King Richard III", 4.
[266] More, "The History of King Richard III", 93.
[267] More, "Epigram 112," *The Complete Works of St. Thomas More, vol. 3.2,* 165.
[268] More, "Epigram 111," *The Complete Works of St. Thomas More, vol. 3.2,* 163.

wolves, but a bad king was the wolf himself who devoured the flock and instilled fear.[269] Alistair Fox has suggested that More stopped writing *Richard III* because he no longer wished to continue "with the lie that his historiographical literary form was obliging him to perpetuate," and in particular, he could not force himself to tell the final lie – that Henry VII had made everything right in England.[270] Furthermore, More's paradox between a good king and a bad king is reflected in the transformation of the character of Edward IV.

More's *Richard III* is laden with irony - that More's Edward IV is not entirely Richard III's moral antithesis in *Richard III* (displaying the characteristics of both a bad and a good king) proves as much. One interpretation is that in More's use of irony, the character of Edward IV actually serves as a kind of proxy for a discussion of the avarice of Henry VII. More knew from his treatment of various historical characters that "the appearance of all human affairs can be turned inside out and reversed."[271] While Henry Tudor deposed Richard III, a perceived tyrant, at Bosworth in 1485, he was likewise guilty of corrupting the laws of the realm. Over the course of several years, his subjects had seen him degenerate into a greedy and paranoid ruler who was consumed with filling the royal coffers.[272] Continuing *Richard III* to the end would have forced More to either write Henry VII as the saviour who toppled the tyrant – which he was not prepared to do – or to engage in criticism of the late king. Ironically, in writing *Richard III,* More depicted a completely opposite transformation in the character of Edward IV as he grew from a "gluttonous, murderous lecher," to a good and just king after having seen the error of his ways.[273] Edward, who was guilty of killing Henry VI's subjects in his quest for the throne as well as a host of other immoral deeds, was only able to achieve goodness through repentance for his actions and the practice of good statecraft.[274] In one of the more poignant scenes of *Richard III,* Edward lay on his deathbed counseling his courtiers on the practice of good government. He warned, "suche a pestilente serpent is ambicion," and lamented that if he had been blessed with foresight he "woulde neuer haue won the courtesye of mennes knees, with the losse of soo many heads."[275] Just like More's *Epigrammata,* Edward's speech was meant as a message to the readers of

---

[269] More, "Epigram 115," *The Complete Works of St. Thomas More, vol. 3.2,* 165.

[270] More, "Epigram 115," *The Complete Works of St. Thomas More, vol. 3.2,* 165.

[271] Fox, *Politics and Literature,* 126.

[272] More, "Epigram 19", 101-111.

[273] Fox, *Politics and Literature,* 126.

[274] Dermot Fenlon, "Thomas More and Tyranny," *Journal of Ecclesiastical History* 32, no.4 (1981), 455.

[275] More, "The History of King Richard III", 12-13.

Richard III about how important it was for a ruler to respect the laws of the realm and to govern fairly over his subjects, lest he degenerate into despotism. These words were so important that the dying king used his last breath to utter them. Thus, Edward exited the play, ultimately leaving the reader to witness as his warnings went unheeded.

According to Leonard F. Dean's study on the literary problems of *Richard III*, More acknowledged that power could corrupt even the most virtuous of kings and that this should be remembered as we seek to judge the kings of the past. More, however, "reminds us ironically that kings too are men with the power to be virtuous if they choose."[276] Henry VII, who was the most recent example of a tyrant in More's lifetime, had chosen not to observe the laws of the realm and had governed selfishly. He had made the choice not to be a virtuous ruler and to give into the temptations of power, essentially becoming the very thing that More's Edward IV had warned against.[277] Thus, Henry served as a real-life example of what could happen to a king if he did not practice good governance – a decline that More had witnessed first hand – and perhaps a veritable source of inspiration for More to draw upon in composing *Richard III*. More could not overtly slander the father of his king, and despite having enough courage to present the condemnatory lines of his coronation ode to Henry VIII in 1509, he allegedly lost his nerve and told the king afterwards that he had exaggerated several verses to give them more colour.[278] Through the character of Edward IV, More could use irony to discreetly grapple with his distaste for the tyranny of the very recent past, while addressing his concerns that it might become a reality in the near future, through Henry VIII. The irony in this was that Edward IV's character arc displayed improvement and redemption, as the king was loved by his subjects when he died, while the real Henry VII suffered a decline and was resented by the people of England when he passed.[279]

Could the paradox between the character of Edward IV and Henry VII be an indicator of wishful thinking on More's part? Perhaps he was lamenting that Henry VII had not seen the error of his ways and been redeemed like the character of Edward IV. Perhaps he hoped that with proper guidance the same decline could be prevented in Henry VIII, who had already begun to display some arbitrary behaviour in the 1510s by reviving conflicts with France and Scotland in

---

[276] Dean, "Literary Problems," 36.

[277] More, "Epigram 19", 101-111.

[278] J.B Trapp, *Erasmus, Colet and More: Early Tudor Humanists and their Books* (London: The British Library, 1991), 42.

[279] More, "The History of King Richard III", 13; Anglo, "Ill of the dead", 32.

order to achieve personal glory. Nevertheless, it would have been far safer for More to explore tyranny and the corruption of Henry VII through a clearly fictional version of Edward IV; this was far more covert than to give Henry a part as the savior who defeats the tyrant only to become the tyrant himself. An additional, peculiar point is that More mysteriously increased Edward's age to make him fifty-three, rather than forty, at his time of death. Thomas Betteridge has attributed this to factual error on More's part, however it is worth noting that Henry VII died at the similar age of fifty-two.[280] This may merely be coincidence, or it may yet be another case of irony among the many examples that exist in *Richard III.*

More's bitter feelings about the extortions of the previous regime, and his belief in the corrupting nature of power, were not secret and perhaps he was worried that his contemporaries would draw a link between *Richard III* and his sentiments about Henry VII. As C. S. L. Davies has written, "we can only speculate about the reason" More did not finish *Richard III,*[281] but perhaps he feared that to publish the history was too dangerous and he thus decided to put the work aside for good.[282] Maria Dowling's study of patronage at the court of Henry VIII reveals that usually "scholars were men of little social standing or useful influence," and it was precisely this insignificance that shielded them from the "tumultuous events of the reign."[283] But by the 1510s, More's social standing was far from insignificant; he could already boast of a career as a functionary for the city of London, and his brilliant performance in 1515 as the official interpreter to Gianpietro Carafa, the future Pope Paul IV, in a commercial dispute in the Court of Star Chamber, put him on the radar of Cardinal Wolsey. Wolsey nominated More as a member of a 1515 mission to Bruges that was "destined to bring him worldwide fame" as it was this voyage that occasioned the writing of *Utopia.*[284] Shortly afterward, in 1518, More would enter royal service as a member of the king's council.[285] While the insignificance of some of the other humanist scholars meant that they could survive the tumultuous climate of the king's court, Thomas More's growing influence would have made it so that his critiques would not pass under the radar so easily. Through *Utopia,* More would attempt to explore the same issues of corruption

---

[280] Betteridge, *Writing Faith and Telling Tales,* 66.

[281] Davies "Information, disinformation and political knowledge", 242.

[282] Fox, *Politics and Literature,* 114; John Guy, "Thomas More and Tyranny," *Moreana* 49 (2012), 166.

[283] Maria Dowling, *Humanism in the Age of Henry VIII* (London: Crook Helm, 1986), 5.

[284] Guy, "Thomas More and Tyranny," 162; House, "More, Sir Thomas (1478–1535)".

[285] House, "More, Sir Thomas (1478–1535)".

and tyranny as in *Richard III*. But as will be discussed, this time he would be far more covert in his critiques of the Tudors.

Utopia is More's most famous work. The treatise was first printed in Latin at Louvain in 1516 for a European audience and has been widely read for centuries; it is the only Latin work by an Englishmen that is still read by non-scholars.[286] The first English translation of More's *Utopia* was published several decades after More's death, in 1551.[287] For our purposes, the focus will be on Book I of Edward Surtz and J.H. Hexter's English translation of the work.[288] Thomas More conceived of *Utopia* on his 1515 mission to the Netherlands and it was also during this trip that he was introduced to Giles through their mutual friend Erasmus.[289] According to Erasmus, More wrote Book II of *Utopia* first, while he was away on his mission. In his 1519 letter to Ulrich von Hutten, Eramus expressed that More "had written the second part because he was at leisure, and the first part he afterwards dashed off as opportunity offered," and this was why there were some inconsistencies in the writing style.[290] J.H. Hexter's introduction to the Yale edition of *Utopia* suggests that More may have actually written the introduction to the work in the Netherlands at the same time as he wrote his discourse on the island of Utopia, and then once he was back in London he was able to write what was left of Book I, including the dialogue between More, Giles and Hythloday, and finally the conclusion to Book II.[291]

In Book II, Raphael Hythloday describes the Utopians and their society with admiration, a stark contrast to a Europe that is "mired in sin – pride, wrath, sensuality."[292] In this regard, Thomas Betteridge has written in his recent study of More's works that the latter was acutely "aware of the paradoxes implicit in his utopian vision," and that "his fantasy of a totally rational world is contradictory and disturbingly irrational."[293] Utopia appears to be the ideal state, one that is devoid of corruption, with a well functioning government and where every man and woman has a trade. "Utopian institutions," wrote Alistair Fox, "turn it into everything that England's

---

[286] More, "Utopia", cv-cvi.

[287] More, "Utopia", cxci, cxciv.

[288] For the letters to Peter Giles appearing in the 1517 edition of *Utopia,* I will be using; Thomas More, *(Open) Utopia,* ed. Stephen Duncombe, (New York: Minor Compositions, 2012).

[289] More, "Utopia", xviii-xxi.; Betteridge, *Writing Faith and Telling Tales,* 75.

[290] Erasmus, "Letter 999", 24.

[291] More, "Utopia", xxi.

[292] Betteridge, *Writing Faith and Telling Tales,* 82.

[293] Betteridge, *Writing Faith and Telling Tales,* 76.

polity is not, but could be."[294] However, several scholars have taken a more pessimistic approach to Utopia by pointing out that the island's many rules simply removed the temptation to engage in sinful behaviour.[295] Despite Hythloday's assertion that the vices that plagued contemporary Europe could not exist in "the Utopian scheme of things," Peter Iver Kaufman has noted that the freedoms enjoyed by the Utopians are actually "hedged about on all sides with rules."[296] Thomas Betteridge similarly argues "Utopians may be virtuous, but they actually have very little say in the matter."[297] The nature of humanity is such that the Utopians only resist sin because of the very absence of those things (brothels, inns or gambling), which might lead men to give into their vices.[298] The rules keep the virtue of the Utopians intact and without them the island might become a beast that resembles the England of the Tudors.

The irony of all of this was most certainly not lost on More, who was clearly deeply pessimistic about the realities of the world he lived in, as well as the people who governed it. *Utopia* reflects these sentiments. The treatise begins and ends with letters written to Peter Giles, More's friend and a prominent character in Book I. More begins by making fun of himself when he apologizes for sending Giles the manuscript so late, since he was "relieved of all the labour of gathering materials for the work" and all he really had to do was repeat what Raphael Hythloday had relayed to them.[299] More then explains that he attempted to get his writing style as close to Hythloday's "careless simplicity" as he could, because then it would be closer to the truth.[300] In this same letter, he reveals to Giles that he is taking "great pains to have nothing incorrect in the book," but he fears he has made some errors. More asks his friend to contact Hythloday to set the record straight:

---

[294] Fox, *Politics and Literature*, 94.

[295] Betteridge, *Writing Faith and Telling Tales*, 77; Marius, *Thomas More*, 167; Arthur F. Kinney, *Rhetoric and Poetic in More's Utopia* (Malibu: Undena Productions, 1979), 11.

[296] Peter Iver Kaufman, *Incorrectly Political: Augustine and Thomas More* (Notre Dame: University of Notre Dame Press, 2007), 170.

[297] Betteridge, *Writing Faith and Telling Tales*, 85.

[298] Betteridge, *Writing Faith and Telling Tales*, 86; Marius, *Thomas More*, 167; Kinney, *Rhetoric and Poetic*, 11.

[299] More, "Utopia", 39.

[300] Ibid.

> I beg you, my dear Peter, either by word of mouth if you
> conveniently can or by letter if he has gone, to reach
> Hythlodaeus and to make sure that my work includes nothing
> false and omits nothing true. I am inclined to think that it
> would be better to show him the book itself.[301]

A first glance at More's letter would point to Raphael Hythloday being a real person and that he is the true owner of the ideas found in *Utopia* – More is merely recording his adventures. However, More's readers, his European colleagues who were familiar with Greek and Latin, were meant to understand the irony in this, since "Hythloday" translates from Greek to "nonsense peddler." It becomes clear very quickly that Raphael Hythloday is as fictitious as the island of Utopia itself. As Thomas Betteridge has indicated, it is absurd for More to defer to a fictional character when expressing concerns about factual inaccuracies, an absurdity that Betteridge points out is meant to problematize the contrast between fact and fiction in the text.[302] More's letter to Giles is riddled with similar ironies and sarcasm; for instance "Utopia" actually translates to "no place," and for More to suggest that Hythloday has been named Bishop of the Utopians by the pope is purposely ridiculous, as is his assertion that they forgot to ask in "what part of the new world Utopia lies."[303] It quickly becomes clear that More is spinning a tale and part of the masquerade is the pretense that he is writing fact, rather than fiction, when in truth he is actually writing fiction to disguise fact. He is amusing himself by toying with his readers whom he expects will catch onto the ruse. In his second letter to Giles, which only appears at the end of the 1517 edition of *Utopia*, More indicates that he has received criticism from a "clever person," who questions the truth of the work after noticing some absurdities in the facts.[304] More, feigning confusion over such accusations, states: "if I had wanted to abuse the ignorance of common folk, I should certainly have been careful to prefix some indications for the learned to see through my purpose."[305] As the reader is well aware at this point, this is exactly what More has done and his learned audience was fully expected to catch onto his quips.

The inclusion of these letters couches *Utopia* in realism while simultaneously alluding to the fictitious nature of the work. More also achieves this by including fictional versions of himself and Peter Giles, engaged in conversation with a fictional character. It is difficult to know

---

[301] More, "Utopia", 43.
[302] Betteridge, *Writing Faith and Telling Tales*, 82.
[303] More, "Utopia," in *The Complete Works of Sir Thomas More, Vol. 4*, 43.
[304] More, *(Open) Utopia*, 195.
[305] More, *(Open) Utopia*, 196.

when More means what he says and when he is joking, but that was precisely his aim. More's intent was not merely amusement; on a more serious note he was also being cautious by creating conditions under which he could deny any responsibility for the ideas in *Utopia* should the crown take issue with them. More does not confront the ills of England head on; rather he places his criticisms in the mouth of Raphael Hythloday, his fictional interlocutor, whom he maintains is very real and still at large.[306] More also achieves this through a fictional version of the long dead Cardinal John Morton, who served as one of Henry VII's trusted counselors and in whose household More had lived as a boy. In keeping up with his ruse, More invites any unbelievers to go find Hythloday, whom he hears is as "hale and sprightly as ever," so that they might get the truth from him. After all, More expressed, "I would have them understand that I am only responsible for my part and not for the credit of another."[307]

Although Book II follows the discourse of Raphael Hythloday, Book I of *Utopia* is told from the point of Thomas More who was visiting the house of his friend Peter Giles in Antwerp. It is through Giles that More is made acquainted with Hythloday, a Portuguese philosopher who is learned in Latin and Greek – but prefers the latter – and has accompanied Amerigo Vespucci on the last three out of his four voyages to the New World.[308] Through their lengthy conversation, which is the subject of the first book, Hythloday tells More and Giles about the many nations he has visited on these voyages as well as the faults he finds in them. Very quickly the subject of royal counsel is brought up. Giles asks Hythloday why he does not enter into royal service, especially since he is capable of not only entertaining a king with his knowledge but of furnishing him with counsel.[309] Hythloday refuses, insisting rather cynically that there is only one syllable that differentiates "service" from "servitude." He also feels that as a learned man he could not possibly make any impact at a royal court, especially since "in the first place almost all monarchs prefer to occupy themselves in the pursuits of war […] rather than in the honorable activities of peace."[310] According to Hythloday, kings are far more concerned with acquiring new territory than with governing the ones they already have, an idea which is reminiscent of Henry VIII's campaigns in France at this time through which he aspired to style himself "King of England and

---

[306] More, *(Open) Utopia,* 198.
[307] More, *(Open) Utopia,* 198.
[308] More, "Utopia", 51.
[309] More, "Utopia", 55.
[310] More, "Utopia", 57; Betteridge, *Writing Faith and Telling Tales,* 83.

France."[311] This discussion holds both a political significance and a personal one for More as he was actively contemplating whether he should answer the summons of Henry VIII to enter royal service.[312] According to Alistair Fox, More was under no illusions "as to the physical danger in which he would be placing himself" should he agree to enter into royal service,[313] and if Erasmus is to be believed, "court life and the friendship of princes were formerly not to [More's] taste," especially since one could "hardly find any court, however modest, that is not full of turmoil and self-seeking, of pretense and luxury, and is really free from any hint of despotic power."[314] Erasmus tells Von Hutten that More could not even be convinced to enter Henry VIII's court, even though by June 1518 More was pensioned as a member of the king's council.[315]

That More did not tell Erasmus about entering into royal service is odd, and scholars of More's works have been unable to shed light on the reason for his secrecy.[316] One interpretation might be that More was not as skeptical about entering into royal service as Erasmus claimed, with the latter perhaps projecting his own hesitations about royal service rather than reflecting the thoughts of his friend. As *Utopia* was aimed at the international humanist community, it is possible that Raphael Hythloday's stance on royal service was actually More's pose as being reluctant to engage in royal service, rather than a real reluctance. In support of this, Cathy Curtis' work on More's public life suggests that given his training as a lawyer and a humanist, entering into royal service was a logical and obvious career path for More to follow.[317] Additionally, More's 1509 coronation ode to Henry VIII is seen by historians as a bid for royal patronage, an odd aspiration for someone who was not interested in court life.[318] Curtis' essay suggests that More may have been motivated to enter into the service of Henry VIII by a belief that he needed to "do what he could to yet guide the youthful Henry in the ways of virtuous kingship."[319] Another reason More may have chosen 1518 to enter royal service was a bull on 6 March of that year by Pope Leo X that proposed a truce among the European powers to enable a crusade

---

[311] More, "Utopia", 55; Marius, *Thomas More,* 155.

[312] George Sanderling, "The Meaning of More's 'Utopia'" *College English* 12, no. 2 (1950), 75.

[313] Fox, *Politics and Literature*, 103.

[314] Erasmus, "Letter 999", 19.

[315] Erasmus, "Letter 999", 19.

[316] Marius, *Thomas More,* 198; Fox, *Politics and Literature*, 103; G.R. Elton, *Studies in Tudor and Stuart Politics and Government,* vol. 2 (Cambridge: Cambridge University Press, 1974), 129-133.

[317] Cathy Curtis, "More's Public Life," in *The Cambridge Companion to Thomas More,* ed. George M. Logan, (Cambridge University Press, 2011), 74.

[318] Fox, *Politics and Literature*, 19.

[319] Curtis, "More's Public Life," 74.

against the Ottomans after their success in Egypt and Syria. This truce, proclaimed in October 1518 as the Treaty of Universal Peace, was significant to early modern European international relations especially given the hostilities between England and France in the 1510s. Curtis points out that such an initiative was only made possible through the intervention of "skilled public servants," such as Thomas More who was one of the treaty's signatories.[320] Through his involvement in the negotiation of the treaty, More may have seen an opportunity to attempt to curb Henry's appetite for war and his designs on personal glory.

What becomes clear from a reading of *Utopia* is that More was actively contemplating his entrance into the service of Henry VIII. He was also disillusioned with the social and political realities of England – almost as though he had come full circle from his optimism for the new king in 1509. This is played out in full form in Book I through Hythloday, who launches a full-scale critique of the ills of contemporary Europe, but mostly of Tudor England. Significantly, More also chose to attribute some of these criticisms to John Morton, who "was among, if not the closest of, Henry VII's counselors."[321] As Hythloday discusses with More and Giles on the subject of his first visit to England, he recalls a conversation about English laws between himself, an unnamed lawyer and Cardinal Morton, whose real-life counterpart was made Lord Chancellor in 1487 and Archbishop of Canterbury in 1486, in which offices he served until his death in 1500.[322] While the unnamed lawyer's role in the discussion is to speak in defense of England against Hythloday's attacks, Cardinal Morton actually facilitates these criticisms by mediating the discussion and entertaining Hythloday's solutions to some of the greatest problems facing English society and government.[323] Morton even appears to favour Hythloday over the lawyer, who talks too much. For example, Morton interrupts the lawyer, asking if they should "relieve [the lawyer] of the trouble" of making his answer. Alternatively, the Cardinal then expresses how "eager" he is to hear more of Hythloday's ideas.[324] This is meaningful, as during this discussion, Hythloday's opinions on the poor state of English laws and government are very prominent and

---

[320] Curtis, "More's Public Life," 75.

[321] Christopher Harper-Bill, "Morton, John (*d.* 1500)", *Oxford Dictionary of National Biography*, Oxford University Press, 2004 [http://0-www.oxforddnb.com.mercury.concordia.ca/view/article/19363, accessed 8 March 2016].

[322] Harper-Bill, "Morton, John (*d.* 1500)"; More, "Utopia", 61.

[323] More, "Utopia", 59-85.

[324] More, "Utopia", 71.

the fictional Morton appears to be actively agreeing with these, and engaging in some of his own criticism of the first Tudor regime.

　After serving in Morton's household as an adolescent and benefitting from the latter's patronage, More held a considerable fondness for him. This fondness is also acknowledged by the fictional Thomas More after hearing of Hythloday's conversation with Morton: "While listening to you," More tells Hythloday, "I felt not only as if I were at home in my native land but as if I were become a boy again, by being pleasantly reminded of the very Cardinal in whose court I was brought up as a lad."[325] Thomas More was not alone in his admiration for Morton; many in England still considered him to be a wise, politic and virtuous man in the 1510s. In fact, as we have mentioned, Polydore Vergil also gave his opinion that the loss of John Morton as a royal counselor was an important catalyst in Henry VII's shift towards tyranny.[326] Thus, for More to use John Morton as a vessel for some of his critiques of the Tudor regime was rhetorically very useful because the former Cardinal was still so well regarded by his contemporaries.

　Through Hythloday's conversation with John Morton and the lawyer, Thomas More reveals his distaste for the harsh English laws under both Tudor regimes. Here Hythloday expresses that standing armies and mercenaries result in the presence of violent and restless soldiers who then go about plundering and stealing in what is meant to be peacetime.[327] Additionally, he condemns the enclosure movement and the fencing off of the common grazing grounds upon which English commoners depended, forcing them to turn to crime in order to sustain themselves.[328] Nobles, gentry and large monasteries that held grand estates would fence off these ancestral grazing lands so that they could raise sheep after buying them abroad only to sell them again at a very high price.[329] "What have [commoners] to do but beg?" asks Hythloday, "or – a course more readily embraced by men of mettle – to become robbers?"[330] Consequently, as is pointed out by Hythloday, enforcing the death penalty for minor offences only encourages more serious crimes as the offender would rather kill their victim than leave a witness behind, especially if both crimes carried the same punishment.[331] "You ordain grievous and terrible

---

[325] More, "Utopia", 87.
[326] Vergil, *The Anglica Historia of Polydore Vergil*, 135.
[327] More, "Utopia", 64-65.
[328] More, "Utopia", 69.
[329] Ibid.
[330] Ibid.
[331] More, "Utopia", 73, 75.

punishments for a thief," criticizes Hythloday, "when it would have been much better to provide some means of getting a living, that no one should be under this terrible necessity first of stealing and then dying for it."[332] Morton is afterwards seen engaging with Hythloday's ideas and even volunteering some suggestions of his own regarding the punishment for vagrancy of England.[333] The theme of the discussion is that the poverty of a nation's people could cripple it, and More, through his interlocutors, believed that it was "not consistent with the dignity of a king to exercise authority over beggars but over prosperous and happy subjects."[334] For this reason, a king should take care of the needs of his people before his own. As this fictional discussion apparently takes place during the reign of Henry VII, More was using Hythloday and John Morton to express his own opinions about the ills of the previous regime. Henry VII, whom More accused in 1509 of having impoverished his subjects, was a king who lacked the dignity of a good ruler.[335] Hythloday's conversation with Morton and the lawyer can also be seen as warning to Henry VIII, that he should put the good of his people before personal aspirations for glory.

Utopia was not only an outlet for More's critique of the regime of Henry VII. In his discussion with More and Giles, Hythloday criticizes kings and their imperial designs on conquest.[336] Here what immediately comes to mind are Henry VIII's renewed conflicts with France and Scotland. J.J. Scarisbrick writes that when the young king took the throne, he had a choice to make between peace and war, but it was also a choice between the old and the new – between the policies his father had pursued and forging his own path through history.[337] In forging such a path, Henry "would lead England back into her past, into Europe and its endless squabbles," and revive the Hundred Years' War with France, so that he could claim dominion over both kingdoms.[338] From 1513 to 1520, Henry was intermittently engaged in a disastrously expensive war with France. While he was away on campaign in 1513, the Scots also attacked from the North, but (as we saw above) they were expelled under Catherine's regency and the military leadership of Thomas Howard, earl of Surrey.[339] In an example, which can be eerily applied to England and Henry's designs on conquest, Hythloday discusses the people who lived

---

[332] More, "Utopia", 61.
[333] More, "Utopia", 81.
[334] More, "Utopia", 95.
[335] More, "Epigram 19", 101-111.
[336] More, "Utopia", 57.
[337] Scarisbrick, *Henry VIII*, 21.
[338] Scarisbrick, *Henry VIII*, 21; Marius, *Thomas More*, 157.
[339] Scarisbrick, *Henry VIII*, 38.

on the mainland to the south-southeast of Utopia. The Achorians went to war to win another kingdom for their ruler, who claimed to be the rightful heir to these lands "by virtue of an old tie by marriage."[340] Hythloday cautions that after the Achorians had conquered the land, they found it was far more trouble to govern it than they had expected: "the seeds of rebellion from within or of invasion from without were always springing up in the people thus acquired."[341] In order to keep this kingdom under his dominion, the Achorian king realized he would always have to keep fighting and keep a standing army, but the true results of this conquest were that the royal coffers were shrinking and there was no more peace than there had been before. The Achorians were being corrupted by war, "their lust for robbery was becoming second nature" and the laws were held in contempt.[342] "All because the king, being distracted with the charge of two kingdoms," lamented Hythloday, almost as though he were warning Henry VIII himself, "could not properly attend to either."[343] Clearly More, through Hythloday, did not approve of Henry's appetite for war, nor his drive to bring Scotland under his control and, more ambitiously, to truly become "King of England and France".

Towards the end of Book I, after criticizing the ambitions of war-hungry kings, More's Hythloday appears to make additional damning and covert remarks about Henry VII. In discussing the poverty of the nation, he conjures the generic image of a despicable, cruel and avaricious king who "was so hateful to his subjects" that he could only keep them under subjugation through "ill usage, plundering, and confiscation and by reducing them to beggary." That a single person should enjoy the luxuries and pleasures of life "amid the groans and lamentations all around him" is not a king but a gaoler.[344] Hythloday's words are uncannily reminiscent of More's critique in the coronation ode of the policies under Henry VII, where he accused the late king of robbing his subjects of their wealth and possessions in the name of his own enrichment.[345] According to Hythloday, any king who engaged in such behaviour towards his subjects should resign his throne rather than grasping onto it by resorting to fear and other despicable means – "means by which, through he retain the name of authority, he loses his

---

340 More, "Utopia", 89.
341 More, "Utopia", 91.
342 Ibid.
343 Ibid.
344 More, "Utopia", 95.
345 More, "Epigram 19", 101-111.

majesty."[346] These are some damning statements to make about any king, even a hated one, which is why they are presented to the reader under a hypothetical guise. More was acutely aware that attaching himself to such statements would get him into serious trouble with the crown, especially since he was well on the king's radar by 1515. Ominously, More's 1518 publication of his *Epigrammata,* containing his brazen critiques of Henry VII, would eventually come back to haunt him, through their invocation by Germain de Brie, a French humanist scholar and poet. In 1520, de Brie actually accused More of slandering Henry VII with his *Epigrammata,* including the coronation ode.[347] While Henry gave no sign that this displeased him at the time, especially given his tepid relations with his father, de Brie's suggestion was a dangerous one. As Richard Marius' seminal biography of More asserts, to send these epigrams in manuscript form to a young and inexperienced king, "at his accession to power and resentful of a shrewish father," was far different than to publish these same lines when the same king was now accustomed to power, still without an heir and "threatened by ominous murmurings about the insufficiency of his lineage."[348] In his *Letter Against Brixius,* a direct response to de Brie's attacks, More dances around the accusation that he slandered the first Tudor king and diplomatically explains that Henry VII had been a prudent king who had uncharacteristically listened to bad counsel in his old age and failing health.[349] As a member of the king's council, More was not about to admit that he had essentially accused Henry VII of being a tyrant, especially given Henry VIII's "capricious temperament."[350] It should then come as no surprise that if More wished to criticize both the tyranny of the previous regime and the failings of the current monarch, he would do so very cautiously by establishing plausible deniability through the characters of Raphael Hythloday and Cardinal Morton. Towards the end of Book I, the former asks More "What reception from my listeners, my dear More, do you think this speech of mine would find?" to which More replies, "to be sure, not a favourable one."[351] Certainly such a speech would not have been well received by listeners of a royal kind, as many of Hythloday's issues were full on criticisms of the policies of Henry VIII's government and those of his father's.

---

[346] More, "Utopia", 95.

[347] Germain de Brie, "Brixius' Antimorus," in *The Complete Works of St. Thomas More, vol. 3.2,* 493.

[348] Marius, *Thomas More,* 246.

[349] Thomas More, "More's Letter Against Brixius," in *The Complete Works of St. Thomas More, vol. 3.2,* 641.

[350] Marius, *Thomas More,* 246.

[351] More, "Utopia", 91.

Despite Erasmus's insistence that even Henry VIII would have great difficulty in convincing his friend to enter into the service of the king, More accepted the position of Lord Chancellor in 1529, replacing the disgraced Cardinal Wolsey.[352] More would fall just as his predecessor had, beginning in 1533 when he refused to attend the coronation of Anne Boleyn. Although this was technically not an act of treason and More acknowledged Anne's new title as queen in a letter to Henry, his refusal to attend was widely construed as a snub against Anne – one for which Henry would not stand.[353] In 1534, More refused to swear the oath of supremacy which made Henry the head of church in England, because he still believed in papal supremacy and his "own conscience would not let him swear."[354] Having taken great pains to cloak his criticisms of the Tudors throughout much of his life and career in royal service, More's moment of overt defiance led him to the scaffold in 1535. On the day of the execution, Sir Thomas Pope allegedly visited More in his cell, expressing to him "the king's pleasure is further […] that at your execution you shall not use many words."[355] Marius' work suggests that Henry VIII was "wary of More's oratorical powers, even on the scaffold"[356] – a fitting retaliation for More, whose many works had been shaped by his own wariness of the crown.

---

[352] House, "More, Sir Thomas (1478–1535)".
[353] Marius, *Thomas More*, 461; House, "More, Sir Thomas (1478–1535)".
[354] Marius, *Thomas More*, 460.
[355] Marius, *Thomas More*, 512.
[356] Marius, *Thomas More*, 513.

Conclusion

In a quest to consolidate his power after a crushing victory over Richard III at Bosworth Field, Henry VII employed dozens of poets, artists and historians at his court as part of a campaign of patronage of European scholars.[357] Through such patronage, the king not only hoped to project his rule as one by divine right but also to disseminate an image of strength and power that transcended the borders of England. As we have seen above, the Tudors were adept at harnessing the rhetorical powers of history.[358] Henry VII commissioned Polydore Vergil to write a history of England that would both immortalize him and his progeny and corroborate images of the king that were projected by other Tudor propaganda efforts.[359] While Henry VIII was less concerned than his father with using history to display the magnificence of his reign (alternatively opting for displays of pageantry and the talents of painters and poets), the young king still recognized that written histories and treatises had the power to influence public perception of the Tudors and could influence the perceptions of future generations.[360] Kevin Sharpe has written that Tudor statecraft involved a reciprocal relationship between sovereign and subject and "whatever the will of the ruler, the enforcement of his will involved a series of dialogues and negotiations." The image and perception of a king "were essential to the exercise of royal authority."[361] Thus, even though Henry VIII wished to distance his own image from that of his infamous father, he still wished to "stress dynastic continuity."[362] Consequently, the various writers representing the reign of Henry VII under Henry VIII found themselves grappling with the avarice of the former while producing a work that would satisfy the dynastic ambitions of their patron.

While the works of Polydore Vergil and Thomas More are difficult to classify as any one genre, they can be considered more generally among a larger body of historical representations of the Tudors in the sixteenth century. As we have seen briefly above, the purpose of writing about the past in early modern England was two-fold: to entertain and to instruct. Vergil's *Anglica Historia* as well as More's *Richard III* and *Utopia*, although structurally different, were created

---

[357] Fox, *Politics and Literature*, 17.

[358] Fox, *Politics and Literature*, 17-19; Sharpe, *Selling the Tudor Monarchy*, 65.

[359] Ibid.

[360] Fox, *Politics and Literature*, 17-19.

[361] Sharpe, *Selling the Tudor Monarchy*, 81-82.

[362] Sharpe, *Selling the Tudor Monarchy*, 69.

for the purposes of contemporary commentary about Tudor England as well as to steer their readers towards a desired moral conclusion. Moreover, these narratives were crafted with the intent to entertain their readers, accounting for the dramatic flair found in More's works and the story-like flow of Vergil's *Historia.* These works exist among the various historically-themed plays, pageants, processions and poems that make up a vast range of representations of the Tudors that either served to amplify the royal image or to counter it through subtle contemporary critiques of the monarchy.

During the political turmoil of the 1530s, Polydore Vergil, who initially started writing the *Anglica Historia* under the Henry VII, censored many of his own critiques of the first Tudor king so that they did not appear in the first printed edition of the work in 1534. Thomas More also censored his condemnations of Henry VII and Henry VIII in *The History of King Richard III* and *Utopia* through the use of irony and fictional characters. This kind of fear-related self-censoring gave way to narratives that corroborated the "Tudor myth" and contributed to perceptions of legitimacy that were so highly coveted by the early Tudors.

That the Tudors were successful in projecting an image of magnificence and power to their subjects and to the world is undeniable. The number of history books, television shows, movies and works of historical fiction about Tudor England that have appeared in the last few decades alone indicate the success of Tudor propaganda efforts in crafting a royal image to captivate imaginations throughout the ages.[363] That the "Tudor myth" survives to this day not only indicates the power of historical works to immortalize people, places and events, it also displays how the political agendas of the past have influenced what was recorded in history books, and *how* it was recorded. This is most accurately exemplified in the portrayal of Richard III throughout the centuries.[364] While Henry VII promoted the legitimacy of his rule, historians writing under his patronage denigrated the image of his Yorkist rival, Richard III.[365] Polydore Vergil's portrayal of Richard as "lyttle of stature, deformyd of body, thone shoulder being higher than thother," with a "sowre cowntenance, which semyd to savor of mischief and utter evydently craft and deceyt" was adopted by William Shakespeare in his play, *Richard III.*[366]Shakespeare perpetuated Vergil's description of a "poisonous bunch-backed toad" whose ambitions for power

---

[363] Sue Parrill and William B. Robison, *The Tudors on film and television* (London: McFarland & Company Inc., Publishers, 2013).

[364] Sharpe, *Selling the Tudor Monarch,* 84.

[365] Ibid.

[366] Vergil, *Polydore Vergil's English History,* 226-227.

led him to order the murder his young nephews in the Tower of London[367] Since then, Richard III's culpability in the murders of his nephews in the Tower of London and his reputation as a tyrant has been debated by historians and the public alike. [368] When Richard III's body was discovered in a Leicester parking lot in 2012, the public and scholarly interest was revived, continuing the debate about whether or not, after five hundred years, the last Plantagenet king was truly the villain that the Tudors had painted him to be.[369] For example, The Richard III Society, founded in 1924 by amateur historians, has taken on a mission to "secure a reassessment of […] the role of [Richard III] in English history."[370] Alternatively, the Tudors have arguably become the most famous of the English monarchs.[371] As the early Tudors knew, history was a powerful tool in the consolidation of royal power and the shaping of a public image - that the Tudor myth could stand the test of time and continues to fuel the modern imagination serves to prove their success in harnessing that power.

---

[367] William Shakespeare, *The Tragedy of King Richard III,* ed. George Macdonald M.A., (D.C. Heath & Co., Publishers, 1896), 37, 84.

[368] Rosemary Horrox, *Richard III: A study in service,* (Cambridge: Cambridge University Press, 1989); Fox, *Politics and Literature,* 119-120; Paul Murray Kendall, *Richard the Third,* (New York; London: W.W. Norton & Company, 1998); Cunningham, *Henry VII,* 2-3.

[369] Patricia Treble, "An interview with the woman who found Richard III," *Macleans* (June 2014), [http://www.macleans.ca/society/the-woman-who-found-richard-iii/]; Simon Cable, "How Richard III had us gripped: King named most interesting historical figure of the past year after discovery of remains and reburial," *Daily Mail* (June 2015) [http://www.dailymail.co.uk/news/article-3128980/How-Richard-III-gripped-King-named-interesting-historical-figure-past-year-discovery-remains-reburial.html].

[370] "About Us," *The Richard III Society,* accessed March 12, 2015 [http://www.richardiii.net/aboutus.php#origins].

[371] Sharpe, *Selling the Tudor Monarchy,* 65.

Fig. 1 The Descendants of Edward III[372]

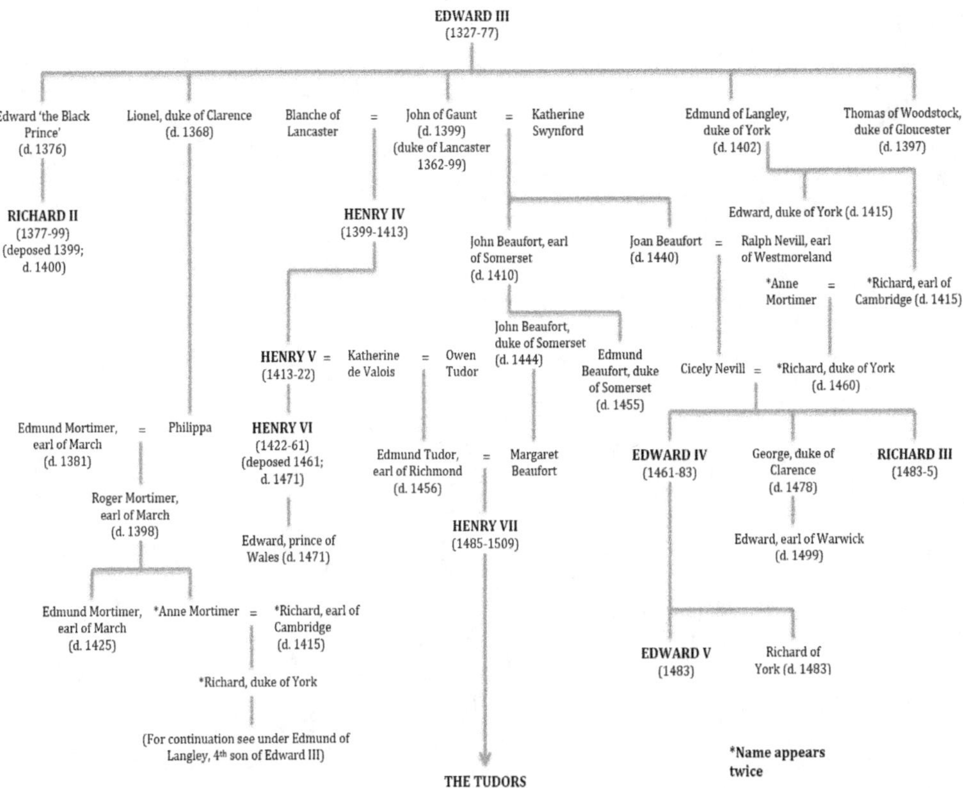

---

[372] Created by author using information and diagrams from Nigel Saul, *The Oxford Illustrated History of Medieval England*, (Oxford: Oxford University Press, 2000), 292.

www.ingramcontent.com/pod-product-compliance
Lightning Source LLC
Chambersburg PA
CBHW072334150726
47998CB00017B/1009